Serpent's Child

Studies in Austrian Literature, Culture, and Thought

Translation Series

General Editors:

Jorun B. Johns
Richard H. Lawson

Peter Truschner

Serpent's Child

Translated and with an Afterword
by
Michael Winkler

ARIADNE PRESS
Riverside, California

Ariadne Press would like to express its appreciation to the Bundeskanzleramt - Sektion Kunst, Vienna for assistance in publishing this book.

.KUNST

Translated from the German *Schlangenkind*
© Paul Zsolnay Verlag, Wien 2001

Library of Congress Cataloging-in-Publication Data

Truschner, Peter, 1967 -
 [Schlangenkind. English]
 Serpent's child / Peter Truschner ; translated and with an afterword by Michael Winkler.
   p. cm. -- (Studies in Austrian literature, culture, and thought. Translation series)
 ISBN 1-57241-136-8
  I. Winkler, Michael, 1937- II. Title. III. Series

PT2682.R85S3513 2006
833'.92--dc22

2005041145

Cover Design
Art Director: George McGinnis

Copyright ©2006
by Ariadne Press
270 Goins Court
Riverside, CA 92507

All rights reserved.
No part of this publication may be reproduced or transmitted in any form or by any means without formal permission.
Printed in the United States of America.
ISBN 1-57241-136-8
(trade paperback original)

Like Water

LIFE had dropped down on my grandfather one day and held him like a fly in amber. Those who knew him would swear that he moved about in this resin shell as if nothing much had happened.

His decrepit body signaled the utter inconsequence of physical decrepitude, of a world whose appearance didn't significantly change with the passing of time. Yesterday, today, tomorrow meant no more to my grandfather than the cracks in the walls of our house, their extent increasing, to be sure, with unstoppable momentum but after decades of neglect taking just long enough to make certain that he, when the house did collapse one day because he had never bothered with its upkeep, would no longer rest in his bed but below ground. What was left of his life he had decided to spend by consistently ignoring so many things, especially his doctor's orders. To wit: he smoked like a chimney, downed five to ten bottles of beer every day, along with as many shots of hard liquor. Myself, in contrast to my mother, never believing that he drank in order to find oblivion. After all, what should he have wanted to run away from? His family background? The knowledge that his compulsive gambling – if indeed it was a compulsion – had been responsible for cheating my grandmother out of her property? Or the fact that at times he was no longer capable of holding back his urine and during the course of a boozy binge simply peed in his pants? So far as I can remember he couldn't care less about any of this. His glassy gaze and the transfigured smile that drunkenness had put into his face were of no concern to a person who had lost any sense of the contrasts and inconsistencies that shape a life lived in the company of others. If as a child I had chosen him for my role model and had allowed myself a form of behavior that might have come close to imitating his ways, I would inevitably have been relegated to the same isolation he lived in. Which hardly bothered him since he was sufficient unto himself and did not pay the world any more attention than was absolutely necessary – the world meaning not merely that which lay outside of himself. There was no difference in the way he behaved toward other people and how he treated his own body. He might scald his hand, drive a splinter into his foot, bang his head, dead drunk, against the rim of a toilet bowl: so what? A normal human response to occurrences like these – such unchanging spontaneous reactions as shock, distress, self-pity – was beyond his range of experience. When he scalded himself, he gave a brief howl, then distorted his mouth as if for his own amusement, and suddenly would start to sing in a way that resembled a loud, artificially protracted yawn, managing to blend his curses with a folkloristic tune: "Ooowwwhsoo-kissmy-assnholishito-holleradullyoh." Then he would laugh and his scourge-red throbbing skin would not for another second have anything to do with himself but rather with my grandmother who would slap an ointment on it while he was looking out the window past the cacti on the sill. She had to get him involved in a conversation, direct his attention to the ripening pears in the orchard, or to the repairs needed on the hay loft in order to prevent him from losing his patience and walking out the door with gauze hanging down his arm.

Grandfather could afford paying little attention to his body since to all appearances it was Death himself who kept him alive. He personified like no one else the all-embracing indifference of death. Any work of accumulating, building, and of preserving things was a waste of time that for him would inevitably play into the hands of nothingness. The older he got, the less endangered did the continuance of his life appear. In the manner of a microorganism he limited himself most of the time to what was absolutely necessary: breathing, taking in food, excreting. Of course, he also went for walks, played cards, watched TV or bought ice-cream every now and then. But there was no way of telling what these things meant to him. Or if they required more energy of him or less than sitting around in the kitchen for one, two hours in an almost motionless posture. Whenever he did get up to go somewhere he would not turn back, not even when my mother came to visit us and was driving toward him on the way to our farmhouse. At best he might stop with a sound of bewilderment escaping him, and then turn around to look at her car as it drove on. He was like water which, flowing in whatever direction with the same indifference, in the end knows neither regulation nor wildness. (Sometimes I'm afraid I'm making too much of a mystery of him when I compare him to flowing water or when I'm quick to interpret any kind of glimmer in his eyes as the spark of life. But when you believe, as I do, that everything is already there and merely waiting to be discovered or invented, then you recognize that the consequence of this notion, life's lack of mysteriousness, leaves enough room for all those mysteries that exist only because one would like to fathom them.)

On days when I overcame my aversion to getting up early I would accompany him at some ungodly hour on a hike up Poppichl mountain. At the start of such an outing I always tried to adapt to him: to his way of placidly setting one foot in front of the other, of keeping his eyes straight ahead and hardly ever looking left or right, of folding his arms behind his back. Since I was ignorant of anything I could use for comparison, I simply thought this to be the appropriate way of walking up a mountain. Since he spoke barely a word before we reached the top, I had again no way of knowing whether any of the things that immediately attracted my attention – birds, mushrooms, paths overgrown with tree roots and branching off of our trails and apparently fading away into the unknown – held for him any interest at all and whether he noticed them in the first place.

The world was not supposed to change during this hike but stay just as certain and available as the time immediately preceding. For to be shaken out of one's sleep by the rough hand of my grandmother meant also that one would be caressed a little later by her wide-awake solicitude, would be combed and provisioned for the hike with sandwiches, lemonade and chocolate. Grandfather stayed away from this early-morning mood of departure, remained indistinct, a phantom that my need for harmony had suffused with a patina steeped in light.

When the morning fog had lifted we would turn off of the boring forestry road. We walked through a sparkling, humming woods of mixed trees until at last we reached a hill and that tree stump on which he would always sit down for his first break. If the sun was shining he would take off his hiking boots and knee socks, unravel his bandage and bare – my childlike enthusiasm for everything gruesome in eager suspense – his left leg, which was riddled with grenade fragments and which always reminded me of a tree trunk that an infestation of bark beetles had devastated over the years. He had been in Russia less than a month when he caught it. Thank God, as he had a habit of saying, at least that saved him from having to go through the agony of defeat right where it had happened; and he also couldn't be taken prisoner or even starve to death, as one of his buddies from Friesach had.

He pulled up his leg which had started suppurating again – as it had been doing since 1942 – and thus blocked out that northernmost suburb of Klagenfurt that was dangerously encroaching on Poppichl. "Them Klagenfarters better stay where they belong," he said. I wasn't frightened by either the one or the other kind of what was festering inside him. Being in my grandfather's company for some time meant perhaps most of all that one would inevitably lose at least a spark of that awe with which one faces whatever horrid or unbelievable facts.

At that time I believed that I could literally listen in on my brain as it worked faster and faster while producing nothing more than an even greater measure of curiosity. I had already learned to value or to fear the advantage that an extra bit of knowledge at school or at home – or any other place where one was invariably compared with other children – was able to provide. Grandfather's dispassionate know-it-all attitude, which as a child I mistook for omniscience, worked as a kind of antidote to childlike amazement, however. It made perplexity rise inside me like air bubbles.

While my grandfather was taking a rest I would explore the near vicinity. At one time I had completely lost track of where I had gone. The stipples of the sun had disappeared from the tree trunks and ferns, and the forest had turned away its countenance of protectiveness and detachment so dear to me. (Though perhaps merely an isolated cloud was hiding the sun.) At such moments the forest was an intimidatingly physical presence to me, a kind of nebulous body that created the afternoon's transition to its inmost nocturnal mysteries – something every child avoided as much as possible, since they were all too closely like the darker sides of human nature as portrayed in the legends and fairy tales of my childhood.

But there was not really any need for me to be scared. I stopped breathing and it took me just a moment to separate his ever so familiar wheezing from the confusion of other noises. His tarry lungs gave him trouble again and discharged one gob of phlegm after the other into his mouth. Those who didn't know what was going on would think a poor old man had come close to a heart attack and needed help, a reaction that provoked my grandfather into coughing up a rude gasp of rebuke.

When my grandfather was in fighting shape, his body produced symptoms by the dozen. Instead of taking care of himself he just, as he put it, threw on another log, lit a cigarette and before anything else took a deep drag.

In the course of time I had gotten used to his ailments – one moment they seemed to have advanced beyond hope and then would vanish overnight – ailments my mother felt to be liens no less burdensome than the mortgages on the property. I hoped the coughing spell which must have been unpleasant if not painful for him would last as long as I needed to find my way back. And I would blindly run through the woods, pursued by imaginary hissing snakes and snarling foxes, and into branches that grabbed me, pine needles that picked at me, moss that was intent on growing rampant around my mouth and slowly suffocating me, as I was crashing straight ahead without looking left or right, falling, crawling, jumping toward the source of this sound. Then the leap across the edge of darkness into the shock of the sleepy light on his face that looked as though it had been made of entrails. His heart was beating blood into his eyes. His diseased liver had given his cheeks a yellow sheen. His lungs made the sprout of whiskers around his lips seem like a charred stubble field. But at that moment of safety regained he seemed to me more alive and full of vigor than he had been for weeks: as though he had the liver of a goose that had been crammed all its life.

Paper Skeletons

AGAIN AND AGAIN his head would droop on the tabletop like a plant that takes only a few minutes to shrivel. The soporific effect of this process made me feel its length to be that of an hour during which one had neither done nor thought of anything in particular. Soon he would have been able to touch his lips to the payment form on which the full weight of his left hand rested. The thumb, index and middle finger of his right hand held a firm grip on one of the ball-point pens he had won at a raffle of a Klagenfurt savings bank. Then he sat up with a jolt, like a prize fighter mobilizing all his strength once more to ward off his impending defeat. I wouldn't have believed it if I hadn't seen it with my own eyes – a payment form could make my grandfather lose his composure. He had put on his glasses and taken off his hat. The skin on top of his head was shining through his greasy hair which under his hat had stuck together in little tufts that, when seen against the white wall in the background, looked like thick, gray strokes made by a brush. I could observe him as he was collapsing into himself, unable to decide where first to put his pen to paper. Even the streets in a city where he had not been before would probably not have offered him as many opportunities to get lost as did the lines and squares on this printed piece of paper. For a few minutes the self-evident truth of his getting old had vanished. What had been left was the torment of finding himself forced to perform an act that had gradually slipped from his memory. Like washing his face, saying thank you. Or now, writing.

My grandfather was one of the old-age illiterates. The few things that had to do with reading or writing he had more and more passed over, with the exception of financial matters such as cashing his pension check, to my grandmother's area of responsibilities. Which allowed him to acknowledge, as a member of Austria's Socialist Party for many years, the democratic principle of the separation of powers in a manner that favored exclusively his own interests: he cashed in while she had to take care of the bills or reminders.

It was also my grandmother who supplied my mother, even long after the latter had moved to Salzburg, with the village gossip of the day, quite often in letters of several pages. For a farmer's wife who, like so many women of her generation, had not advanced beyond elementary school, she took a surprising and frequent delight in writing, which may also be attributable to the fact that it gave her pleasure to write a perfectly crafted hand. But apparently it had never occurred to her to develop an individual way of writing a neat hand, and so over the years she applied to her cursive script the same degree of devoted persistence with which she tended her garden. The result of her efforts in this case were not an award-winning cucumber but a kind of impersonally exemplary handwriting as taught in the 1920s, 1930s that knew neither an excessive loop nor an abbreviating hook. Every single letter differed from the print type used in her primer – which she had taken as her model throughout her life without allowing any deviation – only by that one short stroke with which her ball-point pen connected them, or where the blue ink had used its own discretion and had attached a little belly to an ascetic i in the shape of a blot. No need to mention that her longer missives required the work of several evenings.

Grandfather had given up purposeful reading on the day the first TV set had been deposited in their bedroom and the antenna installed on the roof. So far as I know, that same day was also the last time he had bought a copy of the daily newspaper, until then indispensable for political arguments during card games. For as long as I've known him he has considered reading and writing to be basically negative activities. To him they were like potential traitors – eyewash that stole the face from a conversation man to man. A word or sentence written on paper did not allow you to read a speaker's eyes, or let you tell from the sweat that (for all his smiles) was forming on his forehead if he had it in his mind to keep his word, or if something had been formulated with the intent of covering up the abyss below so many provisos from which there was no escape once you had fallen for them. He detested the various promises offered by the love-and-homeland novels which had become a simply indispensable part of my grandmother's life. No less disdainful were his comments – from one who was a registered party member himself – about election campaign posters and the self-serving stupidity of their slogans.

My grandfather, that old pulpwood hauler, would have been satisfied, so far as writing goes, with an X, suggesting two strokes cut crosswise with an ax. This for him was not an expression of something sorely missing (schooling, for example) but rather a symbol of that taciturn rough-and-ready manliness he admired so much in the heroes of American westerns which, on certain days, sent him home even before eleven o'clock at night so he could watch them in bed.

The only written materials he pulled out from his pajamas in order to look at them over and over – I couldn't tell whether he also read them since he did not, as he did with printed forms, move his lips in the process – were documents that transformed him into something he considered himself to be with an ever heightened degree of certainty after each perusal of these papers: into a man who was irrevocably rooted in the firm soil of his family history.

It was hard to believe, but a leather briefcase he kept in his dresser gives incontrovertible evidence that there had been a time in his life, closely connected with the rise of National Socialism, when he had been persuaded that you could change your destiny if you only tried your fervent best; that your origin was indeed shoved down your throat the way a knife is rammed between your ribs, but that you need not forever be stuck on these facts of life like an insect on a piece of flypaper; that hope was something that might grow even on the slimy bottom of a ditch and could pull you upward. So that this new time, to whose rhythm one was pleased to adjust one's own life without having to think long and hard, may remove the reason for fearing those certificates that would end with the sentence "subject was released in good health and after payment of his wages due to lack of work." (A good dozen of such certificates had been collected in his leather briefcase.) And in further consequence, that the picture of a well-dressed boy walking past him, with his parents holding his hands, would no longer wrench him so fiercely that he had to hold on to his shovel for support rather than use it for turning the soil.

For the National Socialists he had been nothing more than a bastard day laborer – working on road construction jobs or in a sawmill – his mother a farm worker, also born out of wedlock. But that had not bothered him all that much since among the farm and forest workers a stigma of this kind amounted to little more than what the flu meant to them – one had it, but with all the work to be done, did not find an opportunity to be greatly concerned about it. Same as with the mostly undisguised condescension on the part of the farm owners who, however, often enough were themselves responsible for the birth, as well as the death, of a goodly number of bastards born to their female workers. At those few times when he did come in contact, shyly and almost subserviently, with something better – which for him meant just about anything short of the Slovenes – one seemed able to read in his face (the way one notices pockmarks) that he recognized, more to his surprise than bitterness, the absence of his father's name (and with it the man's parentage and character) from his birth-and-baptism certificate of 7/14/1909.

Even though the family he took down from a dresser shelf could perhaps not provide him with any greater security than could a dynastic tree some noble family had painted on their castle wall; even though this family consisted of nothing more than a marriage certificate and fourteen documents notarizing births and baptisms that the district administration had compiled subsequently, all of them adding up to a sequence of officially recorded generations (which, to be fair, extended all the way back to 1777, the year a certain Josephus Schabernig was born) and simulating an origin of the kind that even high-ranking bureaucrats obviously had found important enough to investigate and commit to paper: it was these official inquiries concerning his past that had changed the very way he perceived himself in the present, giving him that strangely uplifting though physically disappointing feeling that, while he was coming home from work to a nearly bare room, he would none the less suddenly find there a horde of relatives, their existence affirmed on paper. The fifteen branches of this family tree testified to a purity investigation that had been pursued with dangerously meticulous care before it turned into officially sanctioned ink. Perhaps the most important side effect of this inquiry for him was the realization that it had been possible to establish the identity of his father, a certain Hugo Resmann, head construction worker from Villach, who, thirty-one years later, had to be hauled into district court at Friesach where he acknowledged his paternity – and thereby helped my grandfather to a new birth-and-baptism certificate, a precious specimen whose special rank among all the other papers was due to the fact that the name of his father was not missing.

There is a triumph hidden, quiet yet reverberating into his old age, behind a pallid bureaucratic statement like: "This is to certify officially that an identification of the extramarital father of the illegitimately born Hugo Resmann has proven impossible because the child's name does not appear in the local orphan registers." If in the final analysis grandfather's family was nothing more than a paper skeleton, then his father, who may not even have known his own mother, possessed even less than that. And above it all was enthroned the eagle of the German Reich – a protector as much as a menace. It sat on his residence registration as well as on a declaration signed in Bocholt near the Dutch border in 1937 and confirming that he had officially renounced his affiliation with the Church; it sat on the document testifying to his naturalization as a citizen of the German Reich (legalized as early as 1935 in Munich) as well as in the membership book issued by the German Labor Front in 1937; it sat on the scroll proclaiming his award of the SA-sports silver medal No. 337.971; and it sat on the violet, green and red disability insurance stamps. People found it nearly impossible to break through my grandfather's reserve, but he became playful and enthusiastic when it was a matter of bending an opportunity to his advantage, even by dishonest means. He probably did not know – I am fairly certain of this – how to accurately assess the deadly threat arising from the movement he had joined. But perhaps he did feel its presence vaguely, being a small part of it himself. And this more likely gave him a sense of pleasure than disgust. At any rate, all I know for sure is that he, like all farm people, buried various types of weapons in his orchard before the Allied occupation, and that my mother thought him capable of just about anything, should he ever use them. As an early Austrian member of the SA, he must have been aware that his recruitment would in the end mean military action, whoever the enemy may be. This, I assume, touched him who loved it when air squadrons formed a swastika against the sky and who was fond of parades in smart uniforms (as the pertinent sequences of snapshots in his photo albums from that time indicate) as little as the so-called Reichskristallnacht – the night of broken glass – that coincided precisely with the time when the competition for the best sand castle at the Bocholt Camp Northwest was entering into its heated final stage and the various groups (including the one to which my grandfather had been assigned) were vying to outdo each other in building the most beautiful mertons, turrets, draw bridges and detachments of garden gnomes.

It might also have been clear to him at this point that the reconstruction of his family tree may well have tacitly implied a deadly threat in case this tree had borne a few pieces of Jewish fruit, or even had grown a Jewish branch. It is safe to assume that he was anxious. But I am sure he didn't tremble with fear as would have been perfectly normal for someone who at that time knew absolutely nothing about the family of his father. Aside from the platitude that whatever may have irked him at any particular time would never have been allowed under Hitler, I have not heard him more than once or twice say anything that had to do with that era.

I would have loved nothing better than to listen to any kind of gruesome war stories he might tell. When, as a child, I had the opportunity of participating in the business of death, everything else became unimportant. My eyes would perform the work of worms with the speed of a time-lapse film: with the dispassionate efficiency of a pathologist I skinned, in my mind, the dead brother of my grandmother as he was lying on a bier. I made him shrivel into a pile of flesh while his soul no doubt had to put up a fight to keep from going to hell. Whenever I was lucky enough to catch a mouse, I derived amusement from the deadly game our cats would play with it. I held my breath, opened my eyes wide and behaved exactly as though I were witness to something inevitable, something I would never in my life have been able to prevent, while the sound of cracking mouse bones (which in point of fact was inaudible among the smacking noises a cat makes) was pounding against my eardrums.

Even though grandfather butchered the animals on our farm, he had little trouble coming to terms with death, treating the whole thing as a matter of minor importance – something that will happen to him just as it did to these creatures. So that one finally got the impression that he was intensely preoccupied with smoking a cigarette or scratching his scalp while between two deep drags he merely needed to take a second for putting the shooting device to the pig's head. Whenever dying took another step in his direction and drove thumbtacks through his heart valves or made black spores sprout on his retina, he did not bellyache. All that happened was that his eyes – whether from physical pain or an unspecified old-age melancholia – would tear profusely.

Now and then he told me stories from his life. They were always the same stories, and there was never an instance during all this time when he would exaggerate or abbreviate any particular detail. Invariably he stuck to the first version. For example, how one day he was unbridling the horse after plowing and the farmer suddenly came through the stable door, yanked the moist headgear from his hand and without a word of warning beat up on him like mad and wouldn't stop this thrashing until his forearm had begun to hurt.

When I asked grandfather if he didn't want to know the reason for this, he merely said: "But why!", mentioning, however, that for a while he had been thinking about sticking the man like a sow.

What fascinated me about the stories he told – aside from their fervent brutality, which in the evening made me crawl under my grandmother's blanket as quickly as I could – was the fact that in telling them he became ever more cheerful and at moments that no doubt were most hurtful to him would slide into a way of laughing that, considering his usual ways, was almost hearty.

Thinking about the eventual time of his own death had not, to be sure, left my grandfather cold – he was simply too egotistical for that. But it had surely left him cold enough so he wouldn't get all riled up about it, just as he didn't become hysterical over the fact that the party to which he belonged was preparing to exterminate a people. His logic in this respect had always been one of bestial innocence. Precisely because a person's skin color or nationality had never been of any importance to him, or with what guilt he had burdened himself, or which guardian angel had guided him through life, so he probably couldn't care less whether Jews, the English and probably even the Carinthians existed or had vanished from the face of the earth.

Things like that could never have enticed him to relinquish his statuesque late-morning position at the opened bedroom window on the second floor – directly in front of him the barn, behind it the orchard and vegetable garden, a bottle of beer on his left side, a plain cigarette between the yellowed index and middle finger of his right hand, and in the center of all this, like a king and queen placed upon the throne of his furrowed and yet strangely youthful face, a pair of slate-colored eyes, their gaze drifting off into a distance all his own, a distance barely distinguishable from the cramped conditions of a solitary cell before whose door one's desire to be admitted alternated with the fear that this might actually happen.

A One-Sided Affair

MY GRANDFATHER, even as a toothless old man with well-nigh no possessions, was still surprised when someone contradicted him or told him what to do. Especially when this someone happened to be his daughter whose life during her childhood seemed to him as usable as a key on his key chain.

The impudent physicality of his grown-up daughter may have intimidated quite a few people – not him. Her big-city resoluteness may have been admired by any number of people – not by him. He believed he could look through this first impression and recognize the unabating lack of equilibrium in her existence, the element of impermanence and the torment. If he wanted to, or so he believed, he was still capable of rousing her into a state of violent anger where she would lose every protective cover that hid her weaknesses. Looking at her made him feel angry, pleased, drained, refreshed, all at the same time. Afterwards he'd quickly grow tired and doze off in his chair though without really sleeping.

My mother looked down on him. She knew his blood was circulating through his body like syrup, his will for a short time seemed pliable like play dough. In her youth it was important not to let these moments pass – as when he came home dead drunk – without putting them to good use because it may take very little time before he regained his presence of mind. And then he would shed, the way a reptile sheds its skin, any form of accessibility, conciliation (characteristics, by the way, that for him described exclusively the body and the emotional world of women), which had taken possession of him as a consequence of his intoxication, and he'd replace his vulnerable armor with a brand-new model.

During those lethargic moments when his constantly watchful, suspicious attention had been temporarily anesthetized, my fourteen-, fifteen-year-old mother would stick a pencil in his hand and get him to sign on all those bottom lines of whatever forms that he would not have signed under any other circumstances. Which means, not without such intractability as resulted from the pleasure my grandmother's unmitigated despair over these things gave him, or not before the due date for a payment had definitely lapsed.

Grandfather's body language which at first sight appeared limited to turning his back on the world was none the less receptive and militant even in the most unlikely places. While the beer he had poured into himself in the cozy company of his buddies among the farmhands and railroad workers did make him droop gradually into a posture of dejection, he could at any moment, so to speak, step out of himself. Every limb and organ in his body would then work toward drawing the attention of all his fellow card players on him. He'd go into an exalted agitation but at the same time didn't want to be distracted by anybody's corporeality or commentary until in the end he was satisfied with the successful recovery of his blurred mirror image in the liquor-bleary pupils of the other players. That he had few friends was due also to his refusal, when it was his time, to be something better than a piss-poor audience for others.

My mother calmed down. Often enough her reaction to her father's provocations was like that of a little child who discovers for the first time – a disappointing but none the less colossal realization – how unyieldingly the world of obstinate, silent objects – teething rings, Lego blocks, doll heads – opposes the fury of its limbs, a fury that loses more and more of its innocence every day. But how well is this resistance capable of inciting a simultaneously destructive and constructive vein in the child's imagination, enabling it to perform feats of the highest perfection! The object of my mother's furious hatred was her nine-tailed lover who entered into her with insatiable desire and used up her ability to love.

Grandfather flourished under the auratic light of his erstwhile tyranny, under the hypertrophic irascibilities he still was capable of conjuring up. His visibly decrepit flesh tightened and a man who for a while needed a cane in order to walk would straighten himself up like a stiffening penis.

He was like a tattered titan. His progressive physical and mental incontinence made it impossible for him to gather all his strength for one final assault. He was vigorous, but the armor for a campaign against that injustice which had allowed his daughter to grow older and mightier, those weapons he no longer possessed. (Which had no tragic consequences for him since, like all gamblers, he was devoted to the strategy of firing off quick shots, of machine-gunning the enemy. It was all-or-nothing-right-now. That was also the litany he and his boozing pals recited like a slurred incantation of the rosary: have at it whole hog one last time.)

Clawing and ripping into one another like disoriented vampires, daughter accused father and father accused daughter of the same crime: "You fucked up my youth!" versus "And you're fucking up my old age!"

Our relatives and acquaintances, believing that this might do some good, would, in the course of years, make various efforts to force these two to put their past behind them, finally. Nobody should be surprised, however, that such misguided attempts turned their perpetrators into mutual enemies of both contestants.

Today I know that these conciliatory ventures were in any case undertaken at best half-heartedly. Our Carinthian clan looked forward to the arrival of my mother at Christmas and at the start of summer vacation basically with as much intensity of anticipation as they accorded the annual erection of the maypole, the beer tents and the dance floors. They knew: If the Good Lord didn't get up on the wrong foot, everything would fit together nicely and father and daughter would climb into the ring together. Which did not amount to an exaggerated hope in so far as an encounter of these two would be accompanied no matter what by an imagined, suggested or even actually thrown punch. One was looking forward to a joyful massacre.

This thing, of course, went out of control and an exhibition bout turned into a heavyweight affair, my mother in the process getting intoxicated with her own, detail-obsessed implacability. She planned her victory, as it were, for kicks, perfectly simulating anger and vengeance. She fought elegantly in an old-fashioned way, knew how to build up to points in the classical style without, however, accumulating too many of them. For by concentrating overmuch (not to say, exclusively) on herself, she failed to notice that her opponent commanded the ability of transforming himself, whenever things were getting too touchy, into a specter, into a nothing of numbing complexity so that she ended up punching holes into the air.

Grandfather did not fight to please the gallery. He took his time, hardly ever landed spectacular hits and seemed to concentrate exclusively on his defense. But when he started to get into it seriously, it didn't take all that long before he had knocked her out as if with a flick of his wrist. At least it looked that way because he didn't break out in a sweat. Again and again he ducked under her right jabs until at last she – soundly defeated – let him be.

My grandmother and I were the only people privileged to stay on till what most of the time was a bitter end. Grandfather – red with shame – had shoved all the others out of the room, if not out of the house. We constituted, as it were, the iron core of fans. The others would not have had the patience needed to pick up on the finer points of this duel anyway. They simply were not insiders.

But it was not what my grandfather did on his own initiative – whether intentionally or inadvertently – but what he managed to provoke her into doing that tipped the balance.

Never was this brought home to me more clearly than on the day he accused my mother of having stolen his savings book. (Which is not to take it for granted that he had one at that time in the first place.) He cussed her out in the vilest language imaginable and charged her with a variety of major and minor transgressions, among them continuous mendacity, repeated theft, undisguised legacy-hunting as well as forgery of documents. Furthermore, he said, she had cow shit for brains and, not least, had always been a dirty floozy. One could tell how much he enjoyed cooking up ever new reproaches.

The old fox had risen from his easy chair whose arms he had gripped like a vise, pretending to be overcome by fury. He was sneaking up on my mother and then catapulted himself as if inadvertently into the heartland of her vulnerability.

Even I, eleven, twelve years old – and thus no longer a child but not as yet a person one would have to reckon with – had seen through his game. To tell the truth: its predictability even bored me a little, since for all their skillful mise en scène, his every move could be anticipated, act after act. I thought to myself: all right, let him play crazy.

It was my mother once again who turned out to be the variable, meaning that her body, her gestures slipped away from her.

The less effort it took him to overcome her aloofness, a strategy she employed rather successfully in her professional life and with her lovers, the more panicky she became. Seeing that she had wasted her best shots – a repertory of let's-get-down-to-business gestures and a scintillating way with words –, she grabbed at whatever she could think of next: "Stay right there! Don't you get any closer, you damned son of a bitch. I know karate!"

For a moment we both were dumbfounded, grandfather and I.

She had angled her arms and squeezed her fingers tight. She had straddled her legs and flexed her knees a little. Her sufficiently determined look signaled that she was ready if need be to separate her father's reddened hobnail nose from his head with one back-hand chop or to ram his third teeth into his frontal sinuses with the help of the high-heeled shoes on her feet.

I couldn't help being reminded of the figure she would invariably cut when, in the evening, she was returning home from her karate lessons (which she quit years ago.) She looked as though once again she had popped too many sleeping pills. (She nearly always complained of sleeplessness.) Her body, distinctly revealing her ribs and shins beneath her skin, was incapable of executing rapid movements and was covered with bruises. Like an exhausted fox who had been fortunate enough to survive a chase, she would immediately crawl into bed. When one saw her fighting (a few unforgettable times it had been my privilege to do so), one simply could not help cover one's mouth and then burst out laughing. When it was all over, her oversized battle dress would hang down from her shoulders like a ship's flag during a lull.

This was the tragic part of it – that he, seeing her standing in front of him like that, was fully aware of all this in a second.

He smiled and simply left this intense little handful of misery, who also happened to be his daughter, standing there while he went to the kitchen for a cup of coffee.

As a child I simply noticed my grandfather's tactics, this cunning variant – country-style – of a field marshal's strategy, without knowing exactly what all was behind it. Today I know why my mother in the course of our own fierce confrontations (I was twelve, thirteen) so frequently tore open the wounds of our mutual family background. One time she grabbed me by the ear and dragged me before the mirror in our vestibule. "There! Look at yourself! Like grandpa! That same devious mug! But I will not let you kick the shit out of me, I swear!"

I turned my attention to my facial expression and was surprised to perceive something for which I can only now find the right words: a proud, nakedly menacing grin which ignored every single one of her words and which continuously practiced negating her existence, if necessary every part of it.

My Land

MY GRANDMOTHER'S naked buttocks were wobbling to and fro like a caterpillar crawling across the ground. They had changed at this moment into an altogether autonomous life-form that even at this stage gave me a foretaste of how things would be after their transformation into the butterfly of all shapely female behinds. And of what these curves would come to mean to me: security, sensuality and – in a state of euphoric distance – the very essence of perfect femininity which, in its perfectness, would also promise happiness and redemption.

It occurs to me also that this was perhaps the first time I had consciously reduced a woman – worse still, one I loved – to one of her body parts. I had cut off her stooped torso, her right arm with which she was leaning against the bedpost, her moist legs and her left arm in which she held the towel she was using to dry herself.

If this had been a situation where I was shooting a film about my grandmother, I could have finished it with this one single shot. For this expansive behind, when in my mind's eye I pointed at it, expressed nothing less than "This is where I am at home"; or, "This here belongs to me."

Understandably, the door frame from which I was observing my hearing-impaired grandmother without being noticed appeared to me as the gate to Paradise – as did perhaps no other place than the lid on the deepfreeze in which the local grocery store kept its ice-cream bars.

That's when she suddenly turned around.

She started shouting – what did I think I was doing,

and that I should get out of here this very moment. But no matter how piercingly she screamed, how startled and aimlessly she stomped her feet, close to despair over having forgotten to lock the door, no matter how futile her attempts to control her large pendulous breasts while covering her shame – no matter, that is, how strongly her angry gestures appeared to express a protest against this violation of her privacy, her face showed no anger at me. Rather, she had to keep her lips most resolutely, inured as they were to sending off commandments or orders and little else, from shaping themselves into a smile, which she managed to do a tad short of nicely. And her pitch-black eyes were beyond her power to keep them in check anyway: they twinkled at me tenderly.

Because it was one thing to protect a child, as morality demanded, from premature, unmistakably sexual impressions, especially when these involved adults. It was quite a different matter to abandon oneself to a beloved other, in all her beauty and ugliness, in all innocence and unspoken temptation, and thus draw that person toward one's own personality so as to become suffused in her. Two people in close proximity who are at the beginning of that process at the end of which physical intimacy will have become an everyday fact of life.

Mind you: mutual physical intimacy. For while my grandmother had all my life soaped me down, washed, dried, and touched me in an innocent way wherever she thought it necessary, I had never before been given the chance to leave the spectator's seat and participate in the exciting game of My-grandmother's-naked-body to which until then only my grandfather had been admitted as a teammate.

My grandmother was a bashful woman. None the less she would show herself naked in my presence ever more often and unabashedly from that time on. Even when her body was more and more going to ruin and she was becoming unsightly – by the superficial standards of a well-proportioned appearance – the silent bond which at that moment had been established between my curious and her smiling eyes was not dissolved until the closeness of death had infested her skin, her odor, her excretions like a fungus and the mere thought of this mush of a body would make me want to throw up.

When I look back at my grandmother's life, I sometimes give in to the temptation of seeing it from the perspective of an ever more noticeable hopelessness and resignation. Until I realize that I am looking at her through the eyes of my mother. The shadow cast by her father clouded her view of everything it had come into contact with. She found it impossible to feel anything but pity for her mother's pride, however guardedly expressed, in her ability to sacrifice herself for others. Because she couldn't see this pride as something other than a woman's quintessential reflex of making a virtue out of the misery of her suppression.

My grandmother's body language exuded the treacherous regularity of time: the certainty that even the harshest winter would give way to another spring. Did she live her life with the contentedness of a cat, far away from doubt and forever closed off from the ability to imagine a different life, an existence in the skin of some other being? Or had she, perhaps as a baby, suckled on the serpent's milk of irremediable bitterness so that one should rather have been searching for signs of some rare sparks of joy in her life and then paint them like stars into a farm woman's cloud-covered sky?

No matter. Her black hair on the fresh cover of a pillow: a bundle of straw dipped into tar. A smile lay on her face like a garland. A good fairy had taken pity on her and in pastel colors had painted it on her features to cover those creases that, as a result of poorly fitting dentures, had in close formations taken up position above her upper lip. Her face, her harsh, ascetic face, always seemed willing to renounce any demand it could possibly make on the world as an inappropriate presumption. Whereas I, ever so clandestinely, know how to derive a pleasure from it which its owner has hardly ever allowed herself to enjoy. That's how it was with my grandmother. I had not been content with appreciating the gifts she offered – protection, selfless love, immeasurable comfort to dispel even the most insignificant worries over things I had more often than not instigated myself, and then again suddenly erupting, well-intentioned severity and remoteness. To possess her fully, meaning: also her body, to roam across it with the means then at my command – my hands, my nose – to survey it like a piece of terrain and to reconstruct it before my mental eyes, as it were, in the form of a map in order to keep it at my disposal for the rest of my life, that is what I had been after. (So give me this bundle of hair protruding from under your head scarf, grandma, like a bouquet of flowers. Imagine it is All Saints' Day and you and I, instead of paying our respects to the dead, pay homage to ourselves – including in this the odors we secrete while we are resting on the upholstered bench after a heavy lunch and then spoon, me with my nose in your armpit, at the edge of your fleshy upper arm with its mosquito swarm of freckles).

 This is what the true owner of a large estate felt: that this is the entry to a piece of the richest pasture land imaginable. Waiting to be grazed by me, it bore your name, grandmother.

 This land under my and my grandfather's feet was so very comfortable, expanding as it did at will in order to satisfy our wishes. Whenever there was anything we desired, be it nearby or far-off, we need not move away from our cozy bench. For as long as I can remember, it was my grandmother who set her legs, as yet sparsely afflicted with varicose veins, into motion for us as if life were a march across endless territory.

She bent over and forced her legs into the smooth black leather of her work boots. She wore a blue plastic apron and a rippled brown cotton shirt. Then she sent herself down the hill for us, rain or shine. Which at that moment meant the same as: We're sending her, never mind the lousy weather, down the hill for us so long as we are sitting pretty. What at first sight denoted a big difference became irrelevant on closer consideration since for my grandmother this distinction simply did not exist. As in general she hardly had any possessions of her own or would think that she needed them – neither any kind of impressive material items nor a strongly developed perseverance when facing the demands of other people. (When long after her death I had a brief look into what she used to call her little jewelry box, I nearly broke out in tears and was ashamed of the suit I was wearing.)

The stations of her life, it seems to me, followed one upon the other with as much unbroken predictability as the beads of her rosary. Given their unchangeable concentration on a central goal, they amount to a perfectly concluded way of the cross, with no specific station assuming greater importance than any other, allowing for no bend, no contradiction, much less a clear break or an intersection where one might have taken a different road. My grandmother who went to mass with great devotion spent perhaps the major part of her life in a kind of imaginary pew, her eyes firmly fixed on her hands as she prayed and listened to them whispering the immutable words: Ask not, bear it!

Matters of domestic duty do not, to be honest, require the use of catholicisms. A wide-open eye is all one needs. The way she went down on her knees; the way the moist brown soil took hold of her kneecaps. She kneeled before the stalks and paid homage to the sun for the fiery-red brilliance of her ripe tomatoes. Then she would pluck them, one at a time, probably thinking of nothing other than her kitchen stove, our appetite, particularly my digestion. (She suspected that what I ate in the city, due to its lack of nutritional value and its chemical additives, was permanently ruining my stomach.) Her weather-beaten hands, cut up by creases as if with a knife, testified to the fact that what she was doing had long become a tradition – that of a rheumatic automatism. One couldn't tell from her face if a specific movement was painful for her. If it was, she would avert her face immediately. And when I praised her expansively for her tomato soup (my grandfather obviously didn't know the meaning of the word praise), her pains, so it seemed to me, had evaporated anyway as if by magic.

This is the attitude with which grandmother stayed in her place and in her time. Other than that, she moved through my life like a specter. But not as a part of my past that was suddenly before my eyes but as something that I felt – even as I resisted it – to be inescapably present. I did at some time get over the fact that there was nothing in Salzburg for me that might have rivaled the absoluteness of her love. Also over her death. But not over the way she had to die. Unimaginable that after her stroke she went on living for close to three more years. That is to say, she didn't really live but merely lay there. Paralyzed on one side, she had spent her final years in bed. In front of her the TV set that was always turned up too loud or not loud enough for her hearing aid. Whenever she wanted to look out the window, she had to pull herself up using a metal bar that had been attached above her bed. Meant at first as a temporary device to help her sit up, haunch at the edge of her bed and then walk alongside it with the support of a three-legged cane, it became an explicit and permanent reminder of everything she had lost. Every day to take a few steps more, or so it should have been according to her doctor's expectations. But nobody was there to help her after the physical therapist had done the amount of work her insurance paid for. Not to speak of the possibility of somebody making her understand that life could go on fully even for a person who was limited to the use of only half her body, if she were to put up a fight. The nursing personnel, by feeding her at noon and cleaning her at least twice every week, did not so much preserve her life as keep death at bay. Women from the village who came to visit her off and on reported that they frequently found grandmother, who valued cleanliness very much, lying amidst her excrement, apathetic or weeping incessantly. (Probably the reason that she herself consistently let it be known that she preferred not having visitors any longer – and then of course couldn't stand it). As urgently, I'm sure, as she must have implored grandfather to push the pot under her behind to keep her from wetting her bed, or to put a fresh diaper on her, as little would he have taken care of something like this. He lived his life just as he had before his wife's stroke – precisely as though she didn't exist. One time, with her lying there defenselessly, he broke her nose – perhaps because she didn't stop crying and he simply had enough of it. This got my mother to consider reporting him to the police for bodily injury and to have grandmother transferred to a nursing home.

Grandmother refused. She expected nothing more of life than to die at home. I went to see her during this time not nearly as often as I should have visited her, and my mother didn't want to face this situation any more honestly. I was determined to let nothing that was going on in Poppichl be connected with me in any way. I must have been exchanged at birth or taken home by mistake. The exciting, interesting type of guy I was working so hard to become could not possibly have originated from these circumstances – so much horror, such ugliness! I still remember that I was barely able to sit down with grandmother, would have liked nothing better than not to have to look at her. Perhaps I sensed that a casual glance would have sufficed to impress itself indelibly on my memory. My recollection paints everything – the bed, the floor, the night stand, the window – with the colors of excrement. The nurse does not show up, the friend who had promised to come gets sick, and grandfather simply does not exist. On the one hand, I don't know if it ever came to such a situation; on the other, I can clearly feel how it must have been for her to be lying there for hours, indeed for days. A yellowish-brown veil has shrouded the light that sustained her life. Urine is dribbling down her thighs, shit is creeping up her spine. I am shaking even though I no longer feel that nausea which would inescapably overcome me whenever I walked up the hill leading to our house and grandmother's body was coming ever nearer. I also no longer hear those screams of which my mother told me only after much hesitation. Grandmother, she says, had literally screamed herself to death imploring me to come and be with her. When she received the last rites, her last thoughts in this world had with unmistakable clarity not been concerned with her sins or God, but with me.

My youthful fury about the end such a life was

destined to have took a long time to calm down. This anger is now turning into a sadness that has a lot in common with laconic sarcasm. Why else do the portals of Heaven and of Hell, whenever I think of my grandmother vegetating in her excrement, of her devout soul in its angelic and diabolic torments, and of her death, look to me like the now clean, now unwashed arse hole of God?

Exclamation Points

WHEN MY MOTHER took me by the hand and let me know that she was taking me with her to Salzburg for good, the world I was familiar with began to shrink. As my mother sat down in front of me and slid her fingers through my hair, I noticed my grandmother disappearing into the bedroom which soon thereafter seemed barely larger than the little room of a doll's house. My grandfather had taken to his heels in time to be spared the screams from my grandmother he had expected. But there had been no screaming and the spirit of my grandfather that would at other times ooze out of every crevice and saturate the air like a cold fog had vanished. All things my grandmother took into her hands grew larger when her probing eyes and then her fingers touched them. The traveling bag she packed for me appeared to be gigantic in relation to the bed on which she had placed it and where I had slept all these years. My mother was standing in front of the dresser. In no time she had gathered what few things she considered usable. Since a new life was now beginning for me, I would get new things also, she promised. Whatever she left behind in the dresser would soon turn to dust. I was fascinated by my mother's presence. By the strength and assuredness she was capable of emanating. With wide steps she paced through the room and bent down from her newly gained height to the toys lying in my corner. Cars. Indians. Legoblocks. The rifle she had given me for Christmas last year. She turned round to look at me and asked what of all this I wanted to take with me. I was too confused to be capable of answering clearly.

Too surprised that my mother who often would become nervous and ill-tempered just a few minutes after she had stepped into this house was calmness personified whereas usually she would light a cigarette the moment she had opened the door, would constantly fidget with her hair and pull at her clothes until my grandfather had enough of it and would say in his rough dialect that this didn't make her any cuter. The rooms were pushing down on her with the weight of the past. Every breath she took, every word caused her pain. Since she was unable either to stop breathing or to refrain from talking back to her father, she had no other choice but to agitate herself into such a rage that her pain could no longer be localized at any one point of her body – her chest, her head – but was everywhere. At this moment she was no longer a prisoner merely of space but also of time and had thus turned into that girl again for whom a life beyond this prison seemed unattainable.

This time, however, space was yielding to her and time was bending her back. My room was cowering before her while my mother seemed to grow taller from this contortion so that it seemed to me as though the door frames were barely coming up to her navel. Nothing about this day was up to her standards and a few sizes too small for the self-confidence my mother was able to muster.

My grandmother must have had a foreboding that there was no way of opposing her daughter on this day. When my mother came up the hill leading to our house, my grandmother silently stood next to me. A final still-shot in a film that was about to end. Even before my mother had climbed the last stairs, life with my grandparents had become a part of the past for me. My grandmother left me standing there and went into the house without greeting her daughter. My mother smirked out of both corners of her mouth but right away smiled again and kissed me. My grandmother served coffee and strudel, acting as though this were one among many other visits whereas the fact that she hardly said a word and did not look into her daughter's eyes proclaimed the exact opposite.

With one stroke my mother closed the zipper of my traveling bag. Her face and an encouraging pat on my shoulder gave me to understand that there was one final task we had to face. Twice she knocked at my grandparents' bedroom door and finally opened it when no answer was forthcoming. My grandmother had closed the curtains and was sitting on the bed, her back turned toward us. The sunlight made the curtain's pattern of gloomy dots shine so intensely that it looked as though my grandmother were sitting before the flames of a nighttime fire. "We're ready," said my mother. "The boy just wants to say goodbye."

My grandmother was holding on to the bedpost with one hand. My mother turned her head to point in her direction. When I stood next to her I wanted to put my hand on hers. But I could not move my arm nor take another step, not forward and not backward.

When my grandmother turned her head sideways and looked at me, the structure she had been trying to build all day, and perhaps many days before, completely collapsed. Its corner posts – her self-discipline and her being prepared for self-denial – were no longer capable of withstanding the pressure exerted by her impending loss. Her face became contorted. Her tears didn't wait to collect in her eyes, but erupted as if from a leaky hose. She mumbled words one couldn't understand and she didn't know where to put her arms. This time her hands found no way of coming together as if to pray as they had so often before whenever grandfather served her a piece of bad news like a bitter pill that she had to swallow. She managed getting up from her bed. She took hold of my arm and pulled me to her. When she pressed my head against her neck, I had the feeling that I had gotten too close to boiling pots and was in danger of being scalded by all the seething emotions and body fluids, of being branded with the stigma of my grandmother's misfortune. I felt her tears dripping on my scalp, heard her wheezing and sniffling, snot collecting in her nose and throat. I felt disgust and couldn't help thinking of the time when I had come to the surface in a moor pond in the middle of a slimy carpet of frog spawn. I tried to slink out of her embrace which I'm sure hurt her if she wasn't too agonized to be aware of my attempted escape. My mother must have noticed my repugnance. She approached the bed. "Come on, mom. Let him be. It won't help. You're only hurting yourself."

Grandmother let me go, got on her feet, and stood there facing my mother. "Why?" she bawled. Because a child belongs with his mother, said my mother and took grandmother's hands into hers. She tried to give the impression both of being conciliatory and of acting with the full conviction that she was doing the right thing. Grandmother withdrew her hand. "Now all of a sudden!" she countered. "Host di do oll die Joah a net bsondas kümmert" (–You didn't mind it all that much these many years.) She should know, said my mother with a noticeable chill in her voice, that that isn't true. And that she had to start again from scratch after her divorce in Salzburg and had to go to work 9 to 5. Who should have watched the child when she didn't have any money for daycare? "What I was able to save I sent you for keeping the boy. I was truly glad that he was with you. And you knew, mom, that this moment would come." "Yeah, sure," said my grandmother in a faltering voice, "oba I hob holt net mäa ols ihm" (but he is all I have).

For the length of a question and the answer following it there had been the possibility that this would lead to a bitter dispute, if not to a break between mother and daughter. Letting me go meant for my grandmother to be left alone with no one but my grandfather. With the silence that could come about when he talked, and with the emptiness he left even while he was still present. All those unpredictable bruises and observations I brought home from playing were for my grandmother like fresh water on the mill wheels of the ever same that my grandfather personified. The life he demanded of her had become more eventful because of me and had helped her greatly to accept the fact that her daughter had moved away. I, after all, was the only one who had been allowed to throw sand into the gearbox of grandfather's daily routine without making him furious. Actually, he would laugh and shake his head over the mischief I was bound to cause. My mother was speechless when she saw that. She couldn't help remembering all the slaps in the face she had gotten even when there was absolutely nothing she had done. It made no difference afterward when she would look at me completely at a loss or defiantly. These slaps were like medieval proofs for the existence of God: they established their own basis and proved their own validity.

My mother and my grandmother looked into each other's eyes. The fact that they had forever been allies whose mutual support had helped them make life under his reign as pleasant as possible also let them overcome the first and only crack in the wall of their solidarity, of which I had been the cause. They embraced. While my grandmother wept I saw that my mother did have moist eyes but was pursing her lips and trying with every muscle in her face to hold her tears back. She was fighting hard to keep her mother's pain and her own sadness about it from overshadowing too much the feeling of satisfaction she was experiencing that day. My mother told me later that even as a child she had tried again and again to run away from home. The few schillings she owned weren't enough to pay the bus fare to Klagenfurt, and she didn't have the courage to hop a train. Since she was also scared to be running around alone at night she never got far enough during daytime not to be recognized by somebody and delivered back to her house. The marks made by the fingers of her mother who had never slapped her before showed on her cheeks like fiery exclamation marks begging her not to leave her mother alone with her father. Sure, my grandmother loved her husband. But first my mother and then I made the difference whether this was easy for her or a burden.

Grandmother went into the kitchen to pack the food for our trip. In one hand my mother held her traveling bag, the other hand held me. She paused after a few words without finishing her sentence and gave me a strange look. Perhaps she was thinking that on this day it was not only she who was insisting on her rights as a mother, but that hereafter also the child would be able to remind her of her duties toward him with an altogether stronger justification than before. The lament over the many kilometers and the child that under tragic circumstances had to be left behind would fall silent and become part of a past which, considering the bare fact of our separation, united us but which, in terms of the reasons for it, prolonged this separation into the years of my adult life.

We stepped out of the house. A sun-dappled breeze was swaying the branches of the chestnut tree and smoothed the worried lines in my mother's face. Everything she had written me in her letters and told me when she came to see me in Carinthia was the truth – but only because she did not tell me everything and because it was an incomplete truth. (And if she had lied now and then as I suspected when I later reread her letters, then the peculiar truth contained in these lies cast an altogether more illuminating light on my mother's personality than the straightforward truth hiding behind them could have made possible.) It was true that she was working 9 to 5 – and hard at that, as she wrote – in a lawyer's office. That she was not making much money and had only a very small apartment. That she saved every penny she possibly could and sent it to my grandmother to spend on me. What she did not waste a single word about, however, was the fact that, shortly after her arrival in Salzburg, she had met at work a very rich and married older man whose mistress she had become. And that in further consequence of this it was easy for her to send grandmother nearly half her salary since this man was more or less financing her life. Her clothes. Her apartment. Her car. And not the least their trips together to Italy or St. Moritz. Not even about these trips did she lie to me – at least not in the literal sense of the word. When she could not come for Christmas or New Year's she wrote that her obligations were simply becoming too much for her and that she had hardly a minute to herself. Explanations that baffled me and about which my grandmother kept quiet, my insistent questions notwithstanding. I put two and two together in a way I found comforting in so far as I imagined my mother's distant life as a struggle that was just as merciless as the one I arranged every day on the prairie of our kitchen floor between plastic cowboys and redskins. A fight my mother had to win primarily in order to survive in the jungle of a big city but which finally was also a struggle about me and in which every little package the mailman brought me had to be smuggled, so to speak, through enemy lines. At the same time my suspicions were growing. The snapshots of herself she enclosed with her letters showed not a trace of such a struggle. She gave the impression almost of gaiety and laughed into the camera. She held her skis as if she were about to use them on a dance floor and not for schussing. She stood alone and with her legs apart in front of monuments and stretched her arms out as if she were part of a jubilant crowd. Since I looked at these snapshots again and again, I noticed that she hardly ever wore the same clothes. On pictures that showed her wearing dresses with a deep décolletage I discovered necklaces of the kind I had seen only round the neck of a princess in the women's magazines my grandmother was reading. When she came to see us, she would hardly ever sleep in our house but in Klagenfurt. "We're not good enough for her anymore," my grandmother would remark without telling me, however, that her rich friend was waiting for her in a hotel.

My mother, when she took me back with her to Salzburg, was not only taking a step toward me, her child, but also a step toward the child she had been herself. What she did would, in her opinion, set me free the same way she set the little girl within herself free, the girl whom her father had sent in wooden clogs to walk with the cows to their winter pasture and who had stepped barefoot into a fresh cow patty and started singing in order to fend off the all-pervasive coldness. My mother believed her entire life that everything I would ever accomplish in mine was due to this liberating act of hers without which I could not have had a decent life. All the estrangement, even the hatred that existed between us for a time were nothing compared to this act with which she had given birth to me – to quote her – a second time. This act wiped out all the guilt she had taken upon herself (if that's what it was, and then certainly without her knowledge) and did away with all the mistakes she may have made while always wanting only the best.

On our way to the car, things were straightening out again. The irritating height of my mother had disappeared. Her gestures, almost intimidating on account of their concentrated casualness, were falling in line with the breathlessness that had come over her as she was walking along with a cigarette wedged between her lips. The skeleton of what had been our barn, now close to collapsing, arose before us. My mother moved on with her head lowered and appeared to see to it that she was putting one foot in front of the other at a steady pace. When I, my eyes fixed on the barn, slowed down a little, she increased the pressure with which she gripped my hand. She did not want the story of this day to take an unexpected turn, didn't want things to change into their opposite, with her, rather than striding past the places of her childhood parade-style, sneaking by or running away from them. She stopped. She put the traveling bag down, took the cigarette out of her mouth and flicked it into a corner of the farm yard. She did not let go of me but once again increased the pressure on my hand so that I had to give a brief howl. Then I loudly called my grandmother. I felt that this turn of events I had so longed for and had thought to be the only right one was in truth the wrong one. I wanted to run back to my grandmother and pulled at my mother's arm. My mother gained strength, as she would so often, from my resistance and this happened whenever she faced any real or imagined resistance from anybody. She dragged me through the gate, ripped the car door open and stowed me on the back seat with the same determination she had used before when she got rid of her cigarette. She slammed the door shut. I couldn't see her head from where I was sitting. But when she raised her hand I knew that she was turning round one last time to say goodbye to grandmother. Grandmother had not taken one step, one word in my direction when I wanted to go back to her. I wasn't angry with her. She simply knew that this was all she could do. As I, packed into red metal and glass, was fidgeting with the car door, I personified the fact that my mother had succeeded irrevocably in cutting herself off from home. She wanted to have me around her but she also wanted to drive away with me as after a victory won in a contest and deposit me at her place like a trophy. She honked her horn twice and we drove off. I didn't look back.

Grandfather had not put in a farewell appearance. Perhaps he sensed that he would be able to walk in and out of my mother's fears and our dreams anyway as if they were houses without doors and he a wanderer through woods and times for whom the distance between Poppichl and Salzburg simply did not exist.

The Maternal Light

THE WOMAN bent down toward me. She was standing on the first step of the stair leading to the upper floor and that made her appear taller than she was. Whether intentionally or not, she more condescended in my direction than came down to meet me. Her skin was transparent like tracing paper. Red and blue rivulets branched out and connected beneath it to form a close weave that had spread across her face like vines on the wall of a house. Her mouth had been arranged to express a patronizing smile. I had barely shaken hands with her when her gaze had already dragged me up the stair and allotted me my future place in the loneliness of her widow's life. I knew right away that the world as I had known it in Carinthia existed within these walls only as a shadow play and that this shadow, when I went to school or to be with my mother, would stick to me and would be hard to shake off. I hid behind my mother. She reminded me to be reasonable. There was no other solution. She had to go to work, somebody had to see to it that I got my lunch, did my homework and did not roam about the streets. But how had my mother hit on her of all people? "I am Aunt Fini," the woman said and passed her hands across my head several times with short and energetic strokes as if she were wiping bread crumbs off the table. I snorted in disgust. "Now, now!" said my mother.

There was a large black wardrobe in my room with squealing hinges. It didn't take me long to notice how much Fini hated this noise. I cautiously opened the door to the living room and made sure that she was stretched out on the sofa, her mouth ajar and her eyes flitting about beneath her lids like a dog chasing its own tail. Then I stood in front of the wardrobe and moved the doors back and forth until their shrill sound had poked a hole into the bubble of Fini's postprandial snooze and had made it burst. Her sleep that seemed to be so sound in truth was an easy victim of my cabal. In no time did I hear her scream, give orders, stumble along the hallway and struggle to get a grip on herself. Like water that was being poured out she would slosh into my room and against me and promise to show me "what's what around here," all the while shouting her anger into my face in moist and bilious words. In order to purge me, as she put it, she stuffed me like a goose with Milupa cereal until I threw up. Thus was restored the innocence of all children which I had jeopardized. As I choked down one Golgotha hill of Milupa after the other, I was becoming that pure child again, at least in her estimation, that babe free of all sins that I must have been at one time and that she wanted to go on seeing in me like a candle inside a lantern. Then she would wash my face with a rough cloth and lead me into her bedroom, sit down on a chair with her arms folded while I had to stand next to her bed and contemplate a picture that occupied the entire wall above her cushions and little decorator's pillows. It depicted a dandy Jesus, his hair undulating as if he had just been given a perm, who was guiding his disciples through a wheat field the way a man might be showing off his newly furnished apartment. I felt nothing. I didn't understand what this picture was supposed to have to do with me. I was glad that I didn't have to kneel down because I felt nauseated at the thought of what I might see or smell under Fini's bed. I only knew that I was not allowed to look left or right, much less give the impression of boredom before Fini had spoken her sign-of-the-cross-like *He sees everything* against my back. Then I would turn round, try to look contrite and nod. Afterwards I had to go to bed even though it was still broad daylight.

In front of the window that looked out into the garden stood a table and a chair. There were two bunk beds at the opposite wall. In the center of the two lower mattresses was a large yellow spot with brown edges. One of the mattresses showed dark-red stains that looked like bloody fingerprints.

My mother had mentioned only the afternoons I would have to spend with Fini. As I was standing in front of the bunk beds, I came to realize with absolute certainty that the black lump of my afternoons would be flattened out like dough to extend into innumerable nights. But even though looking at these bloodstains frightened me to think what all might happen when my day mother would transform herself in her bedroom into a creature of the night, I kept my protests to a minimum. I was mom's reasonable little man who could be sure that mom always wanted nothing but the best for him. During the first night I was so preoccupied with observing the door to my room that I forgot all about my misery and fell asleep.

During my first week in Salzburg I had stayed with my mother. I was surprised. The apartment was furnished with nothing more than bare essentials; aside from the bathroom and kitchen, there was only one single room. But it was much larger than I had expected. No personal things of any kind that may have revealed something about the person living here were to be found on the tables and dressers. I was looking for any one distinctive item. To no avail. Nowhere a photo of me, but also none of my mother. Everything gave the impression of being unused, as if even she had stepped into the apartment for the first time and had left all of her old things behind.

It was her vacation. We drove to the beach and went to the zoo. In the evening she took me to a restaurant. She had bought me a dark-blue velveteen suit for the occasion. During our dinner she distributed pleas sealed into engaging smiles that sought forbearance for my habit of using my fingers in my attack on dead poultry.

I was used to sleeping alone. At the age of three I had been given a bed in the room next to where my grandparents slept. Before that, my place had been between the two halves of their bed. The entire first week I slept in my mother's bed while she took the sofa. The separation of our bodies struck me as something unnatural, not only in the long run but also for right now. In the evening I would lie on my side and look at the wall. My mother was on the phone out in the hall, laughing and every so often checking to see if I was asleep. From the time I had been a baby this was the first opportunity to share a room with her. After she had been on the phone for over half an hour, she pressed a kiss on the back of my head and went to bed. I heard her tossing and turning. Not until the intervals between her breathing in and out became longer did I dare look toward her.

When it came to my going to bed, my mother was as unrelenting as Fini. Also with just about everything else she quickly lost patience when I didn't behave the way she wanted me to. At such moments a kiss or a smile were merely the plastic wrap with which to cover her anger in sweetness without hiding it. It made her nervous that in the zoo I held on tightly to her hand for too long. With her mouth closed, she moved her tongue across her front teeth and started scratching the arm I was trying to cling to. She couldn't stand it for long when I came to within four or five inches of her, looking up at her and into her eyes. She stepped back. The few paces separating us brought back a calm and relaxed posture to her body. She gave me a serious look and then, without the hint of a transition, a smile that was flashed not only at me and the bears splashing in the water behind me but also at those other visitors to the zoo who were passing by us. She enjoyed it when people, surprised by so much friendliness, looked at her in the kind of amazement they would normally reserve for one of the exotic animals. My eyes, by contrast, became more exacting with every day I stayed with her. She recognized that life as she had lived it all these years would be extinguished by the ever increasing and finally unconditional attentiveness my eyes demanded of her. I would inject her regularly with worries and wishes as with infusions that would weaken her immune system rather than strengthen it until my miserable daily routine had become for her a routine of daily misery. The aura of a beloved banished into a faraway realm of yearning was beginning to vanish. She would turn into a somebody fixing lunches, doing the dishes and waiting at the children's playground. If she wanted to go on being the woman she saw in the eyes of other people, she would have to pull out the needle of my syringe the moment it had gotten into her lifeline. There were no two ways about it: She had gone to Carinthia to get me, but she needed to farm me out, keeping me at a reachable distance. If I, instead of entering into her, stayed beside her, I was to be her wearable little sunshine who, at the appropriate occasion, suffused the flourishing landscape of her blond hair and shaved legs with a calm maternal light. As can be seen on one of those innumerable photos her companion took of her on our first and only vacation together. They show me – along with beach chairs and champagne glasses tossed into the air – as part of the stage scenery, a pictorial element to highlight her presence. Wet sand is sticking to my tanned arms and legs. Before long it will peel off me, dried like the scales of dead fish and like the momentary happiness I feel as I embrace my mother's naked legs. I barely come up to her navel. Her large white teeth prove to the camera that even a single parent can enjoy the pleasures of life. Before the mechanical extension of an eye that is devouring her she arranges herself into a buffet that no man can get enough of. It's only at first glance that I don't fit in. Rather, the qualities of what is being displayed assume a clearer profile when one sees them against the contrast I represent. There is her short, low-backed beach dress, for example, or the lipstick mouth she repaints the moment she has emerged from the water; there are the thumb and index finger of her right hand with which she holds the pole of the umbrella. But there are no blue plastic scoops and matching buckets to be found in pictures of this type. No little ditch filled with sea water and fortified with sand levees to keep it even if only for a short time from flowing back into the sea. When my mother packs up our things in the morning to get ready for the beach, she pays special attention to things that – like comic books – make it easier for me to keep myself occupied without her help. A bucket and scoop might give me the wrong idea. But my mother's fingernails are painted red and not meant to plow through sand or dirt. That would be the kind of work to which the farm girl of many years ago has said goodbye for good.

When she retired for the night, she opened the curtains that protected her from the curiosity of our neighbors. She needed the street lights the way a child needs to have the door left ajar so that light from the hall could get in. She had turned her back toward me. Under the white sheet of her feather bed she was lying before me like a snow-covered mountain. I felt the urge to pass across these white summits and to get lost in these dark valleys. But this mountain was alive. It didn't want to be climbed and give up its secrets. When I tried to crawl under her cover, my mother turned round and rolled over to the empty side. When I went at it from the foot of the bed, she pulled at her cover. Since I was kneeling on top, it became taut like the roof of a tent. My mother, half asleep, resorted to using her legs and kicked in my direction, hitting my thigh so hard that I let myself tumble backward, a decision I regretted the very moment I hit the floor. The resulting racket awakened my mother. She looked over toward my empty bed. She got up and for the duration of a few robot-like movements of her head stood in the middle of the room. Then she went to the window, pulled the curtains shut and turned the light on. When she planted herself in front of me, I acted completely dumbfounded and no less surprised by the incident than she. Other than that, I stuttered something. And what could I have said, since the obvious answer, which had practically forced itself on her, was so far from her mind that she had to ask?

After a while I could tell Fini's whereabouts from the noises she and the house made. The moment she had gone back to her bedroom after brushing her teeth, she could no longer sneak down the hall and surprise me because the creaking of the floorboards came through the walls. This would allow me to read comic books with the help of my flashlight. I identified with Batman. He had lost his parents early. Their loss and the resulting loneliness forced him into a double existence which did increase his isolation but also gave it meaning. During the day he acted the playboy. At night he put on the bat mask of the law to hide a face that hatred and despair had disfigured, and to legitimate the excesses of his vengeance. Redemption through love seemed to have been denied him.

In my dealings with Fini I tried in a way to do like Batman and go the route of the mask. In the light of what experiences I had made until then, Fini appeared incomprehensible to me. After I had overcome the shock of my temporary storage at her place, I recognized that her reactions were in fact as predictable as those of a TV set when one pushed the appropriate buttons. I had at first chosen the wrong strategy for getting the better of her. When I donned the mask of insolence and lunacy, she would throw up her hands, run around the room like a chicken about to have its head cut off, and scream "My God, what have you gotten into this time?" She had to tear this mask off my face rigorously if she wanted to reveal again the "sweet little boy that you truly are" underneath it. For all the toughness she used in the pursuit of this goal, she was convinced that we were engaged in a passionate mother-and-son conflict which finally would bring us ever closer.

In the long run she had nothing with which to counter the mask of brazenness and of hatred. When I stuffed myself with her hot cereal, acting indifferent and even flashing a grin while she watched, and in fact made it a point to throw up and to distribute my vomit as best I could across the table cloth and chair covers, until at last she quit this torture on her own; when she made me stand before her foam-born Christ, and I belched into this quietness so that behind me she was gasping for air; when the spanking she gave me exhausted her in body and mind and thus lost its effectiveness and tears were running over her lips without, however, being able to force them open – that was the moment when there was nothing left for her to do but concede defeat. Had she been younger, her ambition to break my will may have been rekindled at this point. But as it was, she had become, slumped into her wing chair, an organic unit of diminishing strength that she had to be careful not to waste. Fini's exhaustion made it easy to notice that she wouldn't have the energy to engage in many more such confrontations and fight them through to their bitter end. If I stayed as two-dimensional as a comic-book character, as tough and unfeeling, Fini would sooner or later have no other recourse but to do what I permitted – including whatever unpleasant incidentals I was willing to accept.

It was to my advantage that for a long time I came home from school full of anger because my classmates made fun of my Carinthian dialect. I would blush every time a teacher asked me a question. Our German class was one continuous country-fair amusement. The German teacher directed his questions at no one but me, riding the waves of an ever renewed swell of laughter. He would shake his head, stroke his white mustache and call me a "peasant blockhead" and a "swineherd." To improve my pronunciation he would stick his skinny fingers in my mouth, move them around and pull at my tongue. During breaks my classmates would imitate him until one day the inspector of schools happened to witness my ordeal, and I told him whose example they were following so assiduously.

Whether her conscience was bothering her because I had to sleep at Fini's so many times, or because she could have me around without my being able to demand her full and undivided attention – following a suggestion Fini made (I had badgered her until she simply broke down), I was allowed to go and see my mother at work now and then. Fini took me to the bus and picked me up afterward until my mother was convinced that I could manage on my own.

The office where my mother worked was on the fifth floor of a high-rise building from which one could survey a major part of the Salzburg central railroad station. When I was still little, she always put me on the window sill of the waiting room. Through the thick windows I saw men in blue work clothes and with yellow helmets who were thoughtfully walking along the tracks, knocking at them and here and there tightening something, while trains were going in and out noiselessly. People who, like the fingers of a pianist, were moving to the right and then to the left, stopped and climbed up the steps of a freight car quickly or panted as they tried to do so. My mother's mechanical typewriter went on chattering in the background as she executed all these movements on her keyboard: left, right, up, down, breathtaking advances, breath catching pauses. When somebody in the station put down his suitcases and took a breather in order to check the times of departure, she stopped typing, took a deep breath and for a moment rested her hands on her thighs. After a few years my mother was given a half-day helper. The mechanical became an electrical machine. Its stroke was softer now, easier on the tendons and yet more rapid. She no longer had to get the typewriter started key by key and push it to do its job, it rather was humming along with electricity-driven willingness. But other than that, nothing about the décor had changed. In the waiting room oviform furniture from the late 1950s, gray felt across a squeaky hardwood floor, two shelves for file folders of closed cases behind burgundy curtains on which orange-green labyrinths had been stitched. On the white wall the reproduction of a Braque still life in a gold frame. In the center of the office two desks pushed together to create a contiguous work space. On its left and right two low typewriter tables that gave my mother a stooped spine and the back pains that until the end of her life made her body keep in touch with her first employment of nearly fifteen years. A few flower pots, a calendar with quotes by wise men, a mirror and a yellowed print of the coat of arms of Salzburg province.

The executive office: rustic Biedermeier that ten years ago had represented sincerity but meanwhile pointed to the malaise of not being able to keep up with the times. Gray felt again. Diffuse, dried-up brown. Pastel pink. Threadbare loden-green. A cap with a hound's-tooth check pattern on the bald head of the attorney who, most of the time before putting it on, didn't bother wiping off his perspiration. "Where in the world is all the liquid on his face coming from?" I always thought when I sat across from him. He was pensive, circumspect. He grinned often, giggled, chuckled and squinted. He reminded me somehow of the little plastic good-luck piglets my mother used to set up in our apartment at New Year's. My mother told me later that one day, when she had returned to the office from her lunch break before she was expected and wanted to get a file from his desk, she surprised him masturbating on his cot. An undressed, gnarled body – like rose-colored gelatin in baking molds. His wife resembled the self-important safe in his office: compact, locked up, colorless. "All he's got left is his own hand," my mother said.

I was a child. He was a boss. And yet in this case the gradient between these two positions didn't appear to me to be quite so obvious. But my mother demanded none the less that I should at least act as though I was respectful of her employer. He was meant to believe that I considered it a privilege when he devoted some of his time to me and let me take a seat in one of the soft leather armchairs that were normally reserved only for his clients. He talked mostly into the fingers of his right hand that incessantly caressed his mouth and chin. Suddenly he threw his head back. I spontaneously expected a splash of sweat, thin as the stroke of a pen, to slap against the glass cover that protected his law school diploma.

Years later he bumped into me on two occasions. The one time, our eyes met in a bookstore across a table with discounted books. He had gathered a considerable pile of books that dealt with the history of the Third Reich. I was looking for cookbooks, picked one up, flipped through it, threw it back on the pile and handled the next one the same way. He, who put the books that did not interest him enough back on the shelves from which he had taken them, looked at me with disapproval. I thought I had noticed a flicker of recognition in his observation slits and was about to address him, when he – hastily, so it seemed to me – picked up his pile of books and walked away. The other time, I saw him on local television among a group of man standing at attention in the cemetery where they paid homage every year to their fallen comrades of the Waffen-SS. I saw his armband. His lips were pressed together to form a straight line of dignity. I saw that he was trying to wrest military steadfastness from his body that was rocking back and forth slightly. His eyes clouded over to an extent that would not, thank God, go beyond what he deemed appropriate. The satisfaction of those assembled was obvious. They knew: the advantage they have over a dead soldier comes from the fact that he can no longer refuse the honor bestowed upon him after his death as undeserved or – with respect to the historical context – as inappropriate. Flags and military tributes no longer tickled the dead and had become a part of that monument which this gathering of old men was in fact trying to erect to themselves.

Heat Phenomena

I CAN BARELY remember the time when we paid day laborers who helped my grandmother in her futile attempts to save the farm. Those legendary days when my grandfather himself pitched in were already talked about the way people talk about apparitions.

But during summer vacation, when I helped out on other farms to bring in hay and when I watched them butcher hogs, I felt as though a projector was being switched on in my head and the mummified, photographic segments of my memory were being reactivated. Various petrified things – blood, intestines, a handgun – which before had been lying randomly and dispersed on the operating table of my consciousness, suddenly assumed an unmistakable connectedness, and from then on I believed I knew with certainty how things had been when we butchered our hogs ourselves. I could, so to speak, observe myself as I – edged by the light coming through the urine-yellow window panes – hung the bridle of our last horse on its hook in the cow shed, whereas in reality it was hanging in the barn, next to the sickles whose broken blades would later lie around on the floor of the barn, partially covered by rotting straw and hay. So that they could barely be seen. My grandmother always warned me emphatically against entering the barn barefoot. Other than that, the sickles continue their rusty Sleeping Beauty-slumber from which I don't want to awaken them any more than I want to bring back the dairy stools or the cast-iron and wooden crucifixes standing or hanging on the walls all over the house.

The scythe and its whetstone were perhaps the only tools my grandfather would use with any pleasure after pulpwood hauling with horses was no longer profitable. He didn't even climb on his tractor unless it was absolutely necessary. I loved his scythe from the very beginning as much as he did, sharing from early on his dislike of a specimen with a metallic rather than a wooden handle. He had developed an almost tender affection for the uneven lines of the hand-carved wood, for blades that stones and underbrush had bent and for their edges that whetting had given a silvery sheen.

With a murmuring swish the blade would slide into the nettles that barred the trail to the raspberry bushes, would circle around the plum trees whose fruit my grandmother every year made into preserves or jam – after spending a good deal of energy on chasing me and my friends down from the branches to which we clung like monkeys. There was no guarantee that we would leave enough plums for her since we adhered to a popular adage and simply ate as long as there was something left to eat. Such proverbial wisdom about the temporal limitation of prosperity and happiness existed in any number of variants. The farmers were afraid of bad luck that might befall them like a natural catastrophe and rob them of everything. They managed always and everywhere – whether by way of an ill-tempered monologue with the announcer of the news or in the manner of a dismal vision of the future during a wake – to come around to topics like the estate tax, the price of animals or the exploitive difference between the interest you get on your savings and the interest you pay on your loans, and they assured each other with great fervor how they are always so hard up financially – even when their new farm implements would not exactly support such a claim. Which is no evidence to prove that there exists an especially materialistic attitude among farmers. Rather, for them who would normally refuse to let anyone know what is going on inside them, the substantial exchangeability of money represented the key to a kind of secret language in which one was able to express fears and hopes as impersonally and casually as possible. A conversation about the crying shame of the estate tax would often enough signify their sadness over the loss of a person close to them, whereas the casual criticism of the Raiffeisen bank may hide their worry over their farm's ability to carry another mortgage.

Once the grass had been trimmed and the dandelions mowed, order had returned to the orchard. The nettles lay at my feet, and I was able to turn my attention toward all those varieties of beetles, worms and snails that had hidden beneath them, looking at them with a still cautious but clearly less respectful attitude, in as much as it took a while before the nettles' villi quit stinging.

Grandfather performed all movements related to work with the greatest degree of slowness possible, even those of which one had assumed that they could not be executed – as for example swinging an ax to split a log – except rapidly. Of course, he gave himself at least two, maybe even three days for mowing the orchard.

After lunch, if grandfather hadn't drunk himself into too much of a drowsiness while he was mowing, we used to play Parcheesi. A game at which my grandmother won with such noticeable frequency that I am thinking these days, if she had been the gambler in the family, we could, instead of losing the family property, perhaps even have increased it.

Grandfather accepted his regular defeats with the lightness of the cigarette smoke he blew all over us in the course of the game until our living room had turned into a veritable smokehouse. Sometimes he coquettishly acted the man who doubts his own abilities, another time the man whose domestic hegemony is being threatened; now he would fly into a fit during a game – but wittily, harmlessly – and then he would exude the malicious glee of schadenfreude when, mimicking the fury of a kicking horse, he threw one of my grandmother's tokens off the board directly before it reached its goal. In consequence of which I had to crawl under the table where, while I was looking for the token, the mixture of floor polish and the odor rising form grandpa's hiking boots nearly made me faint.

At first grandmother would quietly chuckle to herself, but the longer the game went on, the more she lost self-control. Whenever she managed to spoil the long march "back into its hole" of one of my grandfather's tokens, her laughter increased a little until it had spread across her entire body. Emanating from the epicenter of her tightly closed lips, there rose each time the most harmless and least malicious quivers of schadenfreude and of guarded triumph imaginable, and they shook all parts of her. When she was straining to hold back her laughter at all cost she would nearly suffocate, and her breasts retreated deep into her chest; when she couldn't hold it in any longer, her laughter burst forth from her oral cavity like a champagne cork and her bosom seemed to break the wall of her bra.

There must have been a time when she had finally accepted living her life merely as a reaction to the facts her husband set down – more often than not far away from home and hearth. I can't say for sure whether this quiet agreement, as it were, gave her the illusion that in doing so she had accepted her fate of her own free will. I only know that her personal idea of happiness never went beyond what at first sight looked like an extremely modest definition. "To have a roof over your head" and "to stay healthy" were clichés which for a woman, whose very existence was forever most seriously endangered by her husband's dipsomania and compulsive gambling, amounted to the notion that she was capable of steering the course of events, unpredictable as it was despite all one's faith in God, along solid tracks.

It was only during our Parcheesi games after lunch that she crossed the finish line first.

Grandfather had no problems with losing. He could put up with it. Or better: it put him into a happy mood to be defeated in a game by a woman, by his wife of all people, that is to say by an opponent whom in reality he himself controlled and made walk through the underbrush of his shifting temper like a Parcheesi token.

This constellation released in him a veritable torrent, given his character, of seemingly tender affection and loquaciousness: "Do schau, hiatzt gwinnt do mei Weibi scho wieda ... A, was wea i d'n moochn, a woan dos ewig so weita gäat? ... Luada, varreggt's, haut sä mi ä scho wieda aussä ..." (Looky there, my honey wife is winning again now ... what am I to do if this doesn't ever stop? ... Friggin' sonofabitch, throwin' me out again ...)

And all the while he was sliding back and forth on the corner bench, pulling his straw hat back from his brow and then again deep over his face, stroking his three-day-old whiskers, flashing his third teeth, preparing to take them out, holding back and turning his arms, body parts that most of the time are drooping sluggishly or are folded in self-defense, toward his wife's cheeks, her nose, ears, upper arms and not the least, much to the surprise of my juvenile eyes, her bosom. He pinched her, poked her, patted and tickled her and dug the five fingers of his right hand so firmly into her that she cried out in a mixture of pain and pleasure. For a man of his kind he caressed her as indulgently and gently as lather.

I had to remind myself that my mother called friendliness on her father's part condescending and indeed dangerous. "When he is nice," she said, "you have to watch out extra carefully." I would not have been surprised, if she had suddenly stood next to me, shaking her head in resignation. For a moment a touch of that incomprehension with which she reacted to her mother's love for her father affected me also. He was a drunkard who had wasted his wife's inheritance and was easily given to violence. Hidden inside his body while he was physically present, he seemed even more to have vanished into thin air whenever a sunrise augured onerous work or other difficulties. True, my grandmother could come looking for him in the tavern but hardly in the forest – or in some other darkness – from which he might come back to her late in the evening or in the middle of the night, drunk or strangely sober. And pounce on her, panting and rumbling or more like a fainting spell. In the room next to theirs I heard him trying to undress: how he fell onto their bed, how the mattress springs squealed, how he strained again and again to get up and always fell back. I shouldn't have needed to listen in on them to know what was going on. As a little child I had slept in my grandmother's bed and had experienced that even my presence couldn't keep him from intoning a loud singsong and shaking my grandmother out of her sleep. But even if she, while I sidled up to her belly and bosom, had allowed him to push me away and roll himself on top of her: his own weight burdened him down too hard to let him push himself up and down or even just let him move his groin back and forth. Not to mention the fact that, according to dark insinuations made by my grandmother, he wouldn't have been able to get it up any longer anyway. His panting alone indicated how much effort it took him just to breathe. But he had enough strength left – while still half dressed – to try and embrace her and in the process hit me, rather than my grandmother, in the back of my head. Along with his embrace, we were enveloped in a cloud made of alcohol, urine and cow-shed odor, which put an end to our sleeping for good. Grandmother took me to my room. I heard her try at first lugging him over to his side of the bed. Unbelievable that after a reasonably easy day she could laugh about it all or even make fun of him. When she was tired, she just lay down on his side without saying another word. His loud snoring, which the wall between us only muffled, meant that there was no way I could completely escape his influence for the rest of the night.

I think one has to imagine sexual intercourse between my grandfather and grandmother along similar lines. "Like the Holy Ghost," my mother once said, did he always come down on my grandmother. All of a sudden and painfully like one of his slaps in the face when he hauled off quickly and one felt the stinging outline of his hand on one's cheek at the same moment. Too much like an assault and directed toward no other subject than himself, a quick thrust and a squirt, and thus unable to satisfy any needs or desires my grandmother may possibly have had: that was his sexuality. While she was perhaps waiting for the fulfillment of what in her kind of dime novels was merely suggested, never described, he simply was giving in to whatever it was that urged him on. Sexuality for him was probably less a life-determining force than an acute bodily condition that would come and go every so often.

It gave me pleasure early on to secretly observe others during their fumbling in a barn or at the periphery of a county fair. I was fascinated to see how people who in the light of day often barely looked at each other would suddenly start grappling: quietly, hectically and as though they might never get another chance. They reminded me of myself coming home from swimming, always half starved, and grabbing everything on the table with quick, all-encompassing movements and wolfing it down. But there also were couples who only let go of one another when the itch from the hay had become unbearable. The first time I had been offered the opportunity of working my way around a woman's body, I was completely surprised by what I felt. By then I had been living at my mother's for some time and as always spent my vacation with my grandparents.

In my mother's bedroom I found a book titled "How to have sex with a man" which described how a woman, after a successful pick-up, got a man to turn her sexual needs and preferences into his own, and – this was especially exciting to me – what defined the details of these needs and how they could be satisfied. There were stenographic signs in the margins of some pages, obviously added by my mother. Shortly before that time she had started to write a diary in stenography to which she ascribed unbelievable power: "One day, when you can use steno, you'll understand what I mean." (Since it didn't take long before she gave it up, she also had to forgo the prospect of attributing our lack of concord and amiability to my ignorance of stenography). I had forgotten to bring the book with me, which was not all that tragic anyway, since I had as good as memorized the most exciting passages.

After my arrival in Poppichl I let a few days go by before I went to see Gerald, my best friend. During Easter vacation there had been a scrap between us because he had stolen a large chocolate bar from me and had eaten all of it. When I confronted him with this, he blushed, shouted at me and took off. I didn't tattle about him to my grandmother, however, since she would have scolded me for ratting on a friend more than him for stealing. To let him know that this whole thing was passé for me, I wanted to invite him to play the pinball machines at the tavern. He was addicted to the maniac little ball – so much in fact that every day his mother sent one of his older brothers to get him and this brother in turn would catch Gerald's fever and even let his younger sibling take a sip from his beer.

Gerald didn't move. Had he listened at all to what I was saying? I looked into his eyes: they were like semiprecious stones, glimmering immobile in their sockets. His hands, however, were close to being uncontainable: one moment they fidgeted with the straws, pine needles, smarties, little firecrackers, schillings and groschen as well as with the Swiss knife he had loaded into the pockets of his short lederhosen; then he stuck them into his mouth until he had a different idea and grabbed his chewing gum and pulled at it until it snapped. After that he started kicking a tennis ball against the gate of their barn until his mother's frustrated voice hollered at him through the opened kitchen window to quit that.

Suddenly he gave me a very determined look from the side. His body smelled of a morning's worth of work in the barn. At the edges of his lips shimmered a white residue: He always drank his milk fresh from the cow. I sensed that any minute now I was to be the bearer of a secret. We both knew that nobody was better suited for such a role than I, his blood brother. I – a further secret of cosmic dimensions – who last year had solemnly held his dick in my hand. One evening we had gotten the idea of comparing our penises in a state of erection. Result: his thing was longer but rather thin and revealed to my bewilderment a distinct curvature to the right. My obvious amazement flabbergasted him so much that his eyes moistened, and he expressed doubts if he would ever be capable of doing it. After I had calmed him (for which, of course, I lacked any measure of professional expertise), we held on to each other's dick, swearing at the same time never to mention a word of this to anyone. In dead earnest and with a bashful smile Gerald said: "You know what this means." I didn't. Unlike him, who was two years older, I had as yet no clear idea of what conditions and possibilities (including their appropriate practices) came with being gay. During breaks at school the term "Queer dog" was part of the customary repertoire of swearwords. Without knowing exactly what was involved, we associated it with something contemptible that was tantamount to the submissive behavior of a dog.

A secret resembled an animal that was being kept in the cage of one's own silence and that was set free the moment one shared it with another person. It seemed to us that no other place – not the barn, not the attic – was better suited for that act than the corn fields. These fields were the ideal hiding place. Anyone who may have wanted to watch what we were doing would have been detected by the rustling of the stalks. When we roamed through them, just the two of us or in a group, we would every so often stop and listen to make sure nobody was following us. None the less they gave me a queasy feeling. Even though the stalks stood there in rank and file like soldiers, they appeared to me like an impenetrable jungle. Not only could you lose contact with the others and suddenly be left all by yourself, if you didn't watch out. One could even stumble across Death, dark-eyed and brazen, by finding a dead deer that, without a blood stain anywhere on its body, suddenly lay in front of you. The sky and the sun pushed the corn leaves toward each other. The wind was driving shadow creatures across our naked torsos so that it seemed for moments as though the outlines of animals and plants stood out against a chest or a back. When we didn't play soccer or get into a fight among ourselves but had played a trick on other people, we would celebrate our success by, among other rituals, collectively pissing a large hole in a corn field.

The fields were arranged in the shape of rectangles. Since we were old enough to carry the laws of mathematics as a matter of certainty in our hearts, we knew that going in any one direction we would sooner or later arrive at a place where the protection offered by this labyrinth of stalks had come to an end. Then came the village – and the fantasies of children were for the most part no more worth bothering about than the snakes that cars had flattened on the roads.

In the corn fields you could put your hands on someone else's body. A hand would push two, three stalks aside and, as if unintentionally, run across a friend's belly or a girl's thigh. Girls would get on our nerves, and yet it was a special something to have them along. They were on our minds even though we made a huge effort not to show it. It wasn't easy to act as though one was ignoring them while at the same time doing everything to be the greatest in their eyes. They played with their dolls and hopped around in some square boxes that had been cut into the ground with a stick or drawn onto the sidewalk with chalk. Often they would just sit there, sufficient unto themselves and unto their little dresses and little socks and barrettes that always were cleaner and smarter-looking than our pieces of clothing, but also more confining. They stuck to the bodies of those wearing them like a design of the life that awaited them in the village when they had grown up to be women. While we were engaged in our first business transactions – preferably involving pictures of soccer players which we glued into the appropriate albums – they from early on had the real responsibility of doing part of the shopping or helping their mothers with household chores and farm work, things they did with equanimity and a measure of pride.

While the boys and girls in the village always found a place where they could get together, the elementary school I attended in Salzburg enforced a strict separation of the sexes. The concrete grounds of the schoolyard were marked to form a soccer field. One half was reserved for the boys, the other for the girls. During every break one of the teachers would be walking up and down the center line to make sure that girls and boys stayed on their side. Apart from smoking in a dark corner of the gym, between boxes, bucks and mats, our most exciting game during break was running across the dividing line behind the teacher's back and pulling a girl's skirt up. This didn't give one enough time to observe the expression on her face since one had to be back on the other side before her hoarse, sharp scream alarmed the teacher. Of course, one was caught often enough and punished because one had not targeted just any girl but only the prettiest who also happened to be the most condescending. They always stayed by themselves inside the sixteen-meter box and acted as though they were far above such doings. Not one swear-word, no menacing gesture could shake their sealed mind. They retreated, wanting just for that reason, so it seemed to us, to be conquered and thus, perhaps unintentionally, setting the machinery of life-long misunderstandings between men and women in motion. They practiced early on being a trophy. If one had made up one's mind to catch one, even the road to get there was defended by the startled shrieks of other girls and by the teacher's shout to stop it right now. Most of the girls didn't run away. They were proud and wanted to let you know that you were not important to make them lose their cool. By standing still, they gave us the feeling of having accomplished something extraordinary and of having been given the reward one deserved. They would get all excited only when they wanted something. Then their gestures became passionate, and their faces turned red with humiliation for having to let themselves go so shamelessly. A little later – no matter whether they had attained the object of their desire – they could act again with as much indifference as before and look right through you.

Gerald grinned at me and said: "No pinballs. I know something much better."

I knew instinctively that this grin did not belong to him but to his eighteen-year-old brother Franz. Gerald could hardly wait for Friday evening to come so he could get on a souped-up KTM motorbike like his brother and run off to see if "there'd be a little snooze after the booze." A very intense quietness inside my body made me suspect what was coming my way. But since the age of ten, eleven years is still a time in which one's own certainties prefer to dissipate before the adults trample them into the ground of their facts, I chose to pretend that I had no idea what he was talking about.

Gerald took a look at the parking lot of the Museum of Carinthian Agriculture. Cars drove off, others moved into their slots. A tour group in short pants and sneakers was tumbling out of a bus while another group, exhausted by the history of Carinthian agriculture and the obligatory Carinthian cold-cut-and-cheese lunch, was embarking on their trip home. A mixture of busyness and lethargy was hovering above it all.

Gerald was checking his watch incessantly: "Should be here by now."

A woman pushing a baby buggy suddenly tore through a group of tourists. "There!" shouted Gerald, looking like someone who had been knocked on the head. He jumped up, grabbed hold of my T-shirt and pulled me along.

Of course, I had expected something female behind Gerald's emphatically male grin. Someone whose private parts, as rumor had it, were as velvety as a puppy's ears. But I had been counting on something forbidden of the kind that required sneaking up on someone or climbing on a wall. A woman taking a shower without closing her bathroom window, or a couple that thought they were alone in the woods.

Instead, Traudi. A piece of work whose first name had long become synonymous with a popular swearword. Malevolent gossip did not, however, find Traudi to be a lucrative mark in that any manner of viciousness would bounce off her eternally friendly smile. It is remarkable that she didn't seem offended when villagers hissed words like "whore" or "slut" after passing her on the street. On the contrary. It would appear at times as though such remarks had shown her a side of herself that she had not been aware of before so that she would turn round and ask in a gentle voice: "Oh, really? How so?" Those facing her would be nonplused, shake their heads or tap their temple with the tip of their forefinger.

In the end there had been general agreement that she was a little off her rocker – something, they said, one should have been able to tell even when she was just an infant if one had only wanted to. Her widespread condemnation, anticipating the privileges of the Almighty, was slightly modified by a feeling of sympathy which was extended more readily, however, to Traudi's relatives than to her. When one saw Traudi move through the village like a sleepwalker, perform whatever minor chore or go to mass, it was fair to assume that she may not have the cognitive abilities in the first place to recognize a humiliation for what it was meant to be. A sluggish mechanism kept her body moving in a manner that seemed to preclude the need of a will to do so. As soon as one had gotten to know her just a little bit, it was obvious that she had no impulse of emotions left that might have come as a surprise. With automatic regularity her body produced, for example, a smile that gave one the impression she was not projecting it into the eyes of someone facing her but onto a blind spot of her soul.

When Gerald and I were walking with her on her afternoon's stroll to the little woods behind the soccer field, she was twenty-one and had already brought four children into this world. The youngest of them she was pushing ahead of her in a baby buggy, another one she held by her left hand. The oldest two, whom she had had when she was thirteen and fifteen, she had been forced to give up for adoption owing to the mutual pressure exerted by her family and the welfare authorities. Whereupon her smile had vanished from her face for a while, giving way to a dourness that the power of the world around her had spread across her lineaments like scabies.

But her (in truth lost, withdrawn) nonchalance had returned to her with the full force of that determination which is demanded by the desire to forget. Sometimes she was like a ball that was there for no other reason but to adapt to the kicks it had to absorb – and then return to its regular shape as if nothing had happened.

She was glad to see us and that we wanted to keep her company for a little while. As we were walking along, Gerald whispered in my ear, praising Traudi as a serve-yourself kind of a store, as a consolation prize that no one could fail to get and that would get away from no one. If the need was getting too strong and there happened to be nothing else at hand, one would fuck Traudi. Franz had declared that there really wasn't a thing she wouldn't let you do with her.

Even I had picked up on the news that in Poppichl and the surrounding villages she enjoyed the reputation of being something like a challenger's cup. But that was a matter for men or at least for fellows who like Gerald's brothers were very close to being recognized as men. Franz could have afforded, on account of his motorbike and of the grin that his brother was imitating close to perfection, to drive to Traudi's house and to squirt down on his trophy. Such a course of events – I was firmly convinced of this – would remain an unfulfilled promise for us, while in his case it would have made good sense and would have ended in success. (Even if mother's book considered people like him to be scum bags). But we were nothing but children, even if Gerald tried to sell us to Traudi as some kind of "bad-times-edition" of men; as pubescent kids that women would fall back on after their men had gone off to war.

I became a little morose. I was convinced he had been talking too big once again, myself being the first one to know. (How was something major really going to happen, I wondered, especially with her hauling those two children around?)

After a while we made it to the sports field where we saw Hermann all by himself defying the noon heat and his awkward, skinny legs, trying time and again to hit the empty goal. Trying, because his ball was lopsided and had an almost incurable knack of moving toward the right corner flag. Our intent to sneak past him unnoticed had failed the very moment Traudi's sudden exclamation "Ah, look there, little Hermann!" detonated like a bomb in this sporty wasteland. He picked up his ball right away and came running toward us.

Hermann had just finished first grade, never having been a full-fledged member in any of the gangs of five-to-ten-year-old village kids who always were planning some mischief and after school were hanging around Poppichl and the neighboring woods. As far as one's prestige was concerned, it wasn't exactly advantageous to be seen alone with him by other members of one's crowd and, moreover, to give the impression that one was pleased with it. If one recognized such a situation quickly enough for what it was, one could pretend just in time that one was trying this very moment to shake off the bothersome little bug.

For all the contempt in which we held the type of midget Hermann personified, he represented none the less an essential element in most of our adventures. Whenever we needed to get in somewhere without permission, we would send him ahead as a scout. If he got caught and blamed us – usually crying bitter tears – we would, of course, plead absolute ignorance. If something went wrong in the course of a prank, one could take one's frustration out on him.

The most important thing, however, was this: in his naive conviction and – all the evidence of our injustice to the contrary – in his unshakable trust that we were his friends and would not of all things intentionally desert him or lead him astray, he was the ideal object for our need to let our infantile sadism, which arose from a mixture of boredom and curiosity, run free. We forced him to eat live earthworms, hung a string of little firecrackers around his neck and set them off, hid a maggoty thrush in his bed and got him of his own free will to climb walls that were much too crumbly for us.

What we were there to watch was not the spectacle of his triumph over these torturous trials but his failure; injuries he might suffer were part and parcel of our ice-cold calculations. What eliminated our scruple was the fact that we couldn't take him, or any aspect having to do with him, seriously. He was attached to us like a footnote. If he had slipped on a wall, it would have appeared to us as rather an experiment gone awry. And that, basically, was our relationship: we were Pavlov, he was the dog.

There was no way by now of losing him. Even though he had not the slightest idea what this was all about, he threatened to tell our parents everything if we didn't let him come along. In our imagination we beat up on him, in reality we had no choice but to give in to his demand.

Gradually we came to realize that this would not turn into a conventional adventure. It was our hope, secretly, that we, after it was over, would be able to lead the life of giants among the likes of us: casual, meeting every new test of our courage with contempt; infinitely rich in wisdom, in power; members in a cosmic brotherhood; Winnetou and Old Shatterhand.

Our presumption to know that our intent and purpose amounted to an entirely new transgression also caused us concern about the manner and extent of the punishment we were facing if all this ever was discovered. That one could hold Traudi accountable would never have entered our minds since this was unprecedented in our experiences. It was always the children who were punished – especially for what were trivialities when compared with that adult world which in television shows like "The Police Commissioner" and "Crime File XY, Unsolved" came across as more irresistible than horrific.

Traudi leaned against the wall of the little maintenance building like a guitar and offered herself to our clumsiness and inexperience without an unequivocal signal having been given or an inviting word having been spoken. An aura of sticky objectivity had spread around us. A certainty that one was powerless to escape the laws of ever recurring processes.

Gerald went down on his knees and pushed up her tight hazelnut-brown skirt. She wasn't wearing pantyhose. Her flesh was transparent like wet paper: milky, with tender blue veins. I had to think of my grandmother's thighs after she had rubbed Nivea cream on them and of white walls and of the nebulous gleam of rock crystal.

Gerald, his head fiery red by now, couldn't wait any longer and yanked her skirt almost up to her navel, whereupon she chided him without any harshness: "Hey, don't rip anything!"

Much to our surprise which turned into a moment's petrification, Traudi wasn't wearing panties: something we had never before been able to perceive, and indeed to think possible, in connection with an adult person.

Traudi giggled: "I must've lost'm somewhere."

After a while I turned round to see if somebody might watch or have followed us. I still remember how I wished then to be capable of removing Traudi's pussy from the shadow cast by the little house and lay it in front of me across the hot flagstone and to watch as it contracted in the heat or gave off sparks. I wanted to sit down in front of it the way I face a math problem or the topic for a composition.

Instead, it was Gerald again who took the initiative and thrust out his hand. With clumsy fingers he poked around in Traudi's pubic hair and kneaded her labia the same way we tore little pieces out of loafs of bread and shaped them into pellets that we would shoot at each other.

"Hey, not so rough, you knucklehead!" Traudi promptly protested and pushed him off. He stumbled backward and then stood there as if rooted to the ground.

When I approached her lap, her body dissolved into an afternoon's heat apparition. I had decided to let my expertise sparkle as my mind was flipping like furious through my mother's guidebook. And in point of fact I did manage to follow somewhat correctly the instructions to be found in a chapter titled "A slip of the tongue" as I treated Traudi's body. At a moment when a grown-up woman allowed me for the first time to share her sexuality as a partner, I behaved before the incomprehensibility of her naked body like a do-it-yourselfer before some sheets of veneer, screws and hinges, unable to turn his eyes away from the service manual to see the obvious.

Traudi did not realize that I was playing a double game when I retreated into the safety of hackneyed phrases and statistics. Apparently she noticed nothing but the playful maturity with which I touched her. As I was stroking her pubic hair with the back of my hand. As I gently unfolded her labia that stuck together like Siamese twins, separating them as if they were pieces of parchment that the slightest gust of wind might turn to dust. Then she took my hand, moved it aside and pulled my head close. She spoke to me through her body. She bent her knees a little and pressed her pulsating pussy against my lips: it was beating at my tongue like a racing heart, like a clock out of control. Traudi mumbled something about the unexpected satisfaction I was giving her. She, who until then had stood on her left leg and had pressed the sole of her right foot against the wall, now stood before me with both of her legs apart and on the ground. I could feel her looking at the back of my neck when I decided to advance farther into her body than I had ever thought possible.

By pressing her womb against me and offering herself to me like an opened book, she had confirmed my assumption that until now I had understood and converted everything correctly. I could have soared into the air. Did I feel like Siegfried who had bathed in the dragon's blood? Did one not, after such a great success so early in life, have a right to suffer fewer performance anxieties later on, to spill a smaller quantity of one's heart's blood? I was ready to close the book in my head. And also the one on my lips, my tongue and in my nose. Because I had meanwhile bent forward and had embraced her thighs with both arms. I had opened my mouth wide so that her vagina filled my oral cavity like a scoop of ice-cream; so that I (without knowing it absolutely for sure) was sailing round her clitoris with the tip of my tongue and, by changing the nautical category, was licking her crack back and forth with the steady strokes of an oarsman. I thought I heard a restrained but excited gurgling even though today this whole scene makes me think rather of a cow slavering over a salt lick.

At last I had gotten to a point where my facial muscles were no less exhausted than my childlike perceptive faculties. I sensed that whatever might come after this indubitably titanic accomplishment would inevitably end in impotent failure and disappointment.

Last but not least I also had absorbed the specific scents of Traudi's pussy. This peculiar mixture of marshland and sickroom, overlaid with a tart though not in the least repulsive pinch of piss that tweaked the mucous membranes in my nose like delicate needles, had changed into something higher – a destination – that encompassed the scent and taste of Traudi's pussy: the wish to be fucked.

A wish, it turned out, I wasn't able to fulfill after all.

I had a very strong need afterward to withdraw and not to soil what I had experienced with the dirty words we – Gerald more than anyone else – would inevitably find to describe what had happened. The moment I touched her down there with my tongue, it had become immaterial that she was obviously allowing someone to finger her. Later on Gerald (in trying to change his envy into contempt) would impress her existence as the village whore so insistently on my memory that this couldn't but leave a shallow aftertaste.

My anxieties were unfounded. Gerald had found his victim whom he used to work off his anger at having failed to emerge as the hero of the day. He had focused his expressionless eyes like a rifle's scope on Hermann. Within a second I saw it all before me: how he would find and bare Hermann's weak point; how he would stir in it with a poker, how he would make him cry; and how he would finally cure him of his screams by breaking what was a fainthearted will in the first place and by strangling his innocent soul. This, to be sure, was the unspoken, cruel pact Hermann had entered into before he could become a member of our gang at his age. He was the one we threw to the gods and the adults in order to gain their favor or to assuage them. He was, so to speak, the scratching post at which we clawed with the talons both of our high spirits and our ill temper.

Hermann stood there as still as a shrub in dead air. Only the fact that he was human distinguished him superficially from the bushes behind him. His eyes were glued to Traudi's naked abdomen as if to provide the panties she wasn't wearing.

"Hey, Hermann!" Gerald's voice interrupted Hermann's reverent attention, "you haven't had your turn yet!"

He jumped forward and closed both his hands around Hermann's left arm. Then he put a deadlock on him and tripped him up so that Hermann went down on his knees, his nose directly in front of Traudi's crotch. "Let's go, 's go!" commanded Gerald exactly as he did when in the evening he drove their cows from the pasture into the barn.

I stayed back and watched from the side as the puzzle game of Hermann's illuminated face fell apart. There was no sense in trying to look for the individual pieces or in filling the gaps temporarily because something was breaking out all over Hermann. Tears, cold sweat and spittle made his freckled face look like a sunburn that is being treated with a thick ointment. He screamed and stomped his feet as if his life were at stake, as if his mother were about to abandon him for all times in the wilderness. Something he would not have done in his right mind since he knew all too well, as we all did, that such behavior was only going to intensify Gerald's cruel streak.

The moment Gerald pressed Hermann's head against Traudi's pussy, I saw Hermann close his eyes and once more fall into the black hole of our double-edged friendship. I don't know for sure what had happened to him there, what had been broken inside him or had been deadened. I know only that he did come back out on the other end without having become dematerialized or turned into an emotional cripple. After this kind of cruelty he simply avoided us for a while – until one day he came toward us during a soccer game as if nothing had happened and took over the unpopular position of halfback. That's how things went on until he reached puberty.

I have no recollection of how we parted on that day: whether we took off hastily or walked with Traudi for a little while; whether we talked to each other about it or silently moved on side by side as we had done so often immediately after some mischief – I can't remember any of this, nor do I have a clearer idea about what Traudi's children had been doing: did they keep themselves occupied on their own, or had they been watching us the whole time we were busy with their mother.

One day after I had turned thirteen, I was lying in front of the TV set with Manuela, an eleven-year-old girl with whom I bothered to spend time only when I was very bored. Just as we were testing out all the programs in my collection of video games, she abruptly got up to leave but stopped right at the door and turned around. She came back, planted herself directly in front of me and pulled her jogging pants down to her knees in one quick move. Her whitish nakedness repelled me at first sight. And yet I reached out for her and held her labia between my fingers.

I looked up at her but didn't find her eyes which – so I had expected – should have rested on the places where I touched her. Instead, she was staring at a picture on the wall. Her mouth was open, saliva began collecting in one corner of it. She gave the impression of suddenly having been robbed of her senses. I felt as though my vocal cords had been severed, my ear drums torn apart. The luminescence of her eyes was gone, her self seemed extinguished: a mirror of the outside world without a will of her own.

I was startled because suddenly I saw Traudi's face before me: the way her eyes, while Gerald was pawing her, had been fixed on the large, red-and-white painted sign of the A & O depot on the other side of the railroad crossing; saw the way she had rammed her half-naked body into the earth before me, imbued with an equal measure of indifference, magnanimity and feeblemindedness.

In my recollections I won't allow myself to be deceived any longer by her smile or by her encouraging comments. As time went by, the latter appeared to me anyway to have sounded more like the signals given off by a measuring device than like a part of spontaneous human language.

Whoever may think that these oppressive associations had kept me from sending the tip of my tongue into a circuit around Manuela's clitoris is mistaken, especially since this experience became the start of that intimacy which over years and kilometers, through illnesses and after other partners made us search out and find one another again and again.

Years later my mother told me that Traudi had killed herself and that her first child had been fathered by her own father. In those days I was determined at all cost not to become a prisoner of my own childhood like my mother, and so I forced myself to react to all this as casually as possible. Did Traudi want to offer herself at the lowest cut-rate price until nobody thought it worth his while any longer to possess her and she would finally be left alone? Or did she want to become completely apathetic and immune to any form of pain? Whatever. A wrong may simply have reached its terribly logical conclusion. In the end the gutter press too came down on her abused life and made a bonfire of what was left of it.

The Falcon

MY GRANDPARENTS' HOUSE had defied wind and weather for God only knows how long. It gave you the impression that a car that didn't quite make the curve would have been all it took to make it come crashing down. People say it was during the 1950s that my grandfather did repairs on the outside plaster for the last time. Since our place was located not too far from the historic center of a town which owing to its Gothic church had a certain attraction for tourists, there would appear in our mailbox at regular intervals official reminders from the Poppichl Community Council that buildings should be in conformance with the well cared-for appearance of the town as a whole. In this matter I fully sided with the mayor, for the single reason that the desolate condition of our place – house, sheds, barn – unmistakably showed up a fact that I, who was becoming ever more aware of my role within a social construct, could only look upon as a source of shame: the fact that we were poor, that just about everything belonged to the bank. And so there was no call to invest a great deal of effort in the upkeep of the property. In the end, my grandparents had nothing left but the right of residence for life which my grandfather gave up after his wife's death in return for a monthly allowance to supplement his pension. But there was no cause to find fault with the interior of the house. Grandmother wasted a major part of her energy during her final years, when she was still able to work, with keeping the rooms in such good shape that one might have thought she was planning to show them to sightseers and charge admission.

After a period of anger and defiance I had to accept at last that it was simply impossible for my grandparents to buy me the toys I had set my mind on having – always the latest and most expensive ones, of course. I would press my head against the window of a toy store in Klagenfurt until the glass fogged over from my breathing in and out and the toys behind it disappeared to the same extent that they made me see how poor we were in comparison with other families in the village. And how little, again when compared to those around us, we were a family to begin with. Perhaps this was the root cause of the peculiar timidity and aggressiveness I felt in my encounters with other children. The hopelessness that overcame me when Gerald's father gave him money for the fair and, along with a reminder not to drink too much, a friendly slap on the shoulder. When I stayed at my friends' houses to play, their toys were also the objects of unfulfillable yearnings for me so that I was in a constant state of readiness to be invited to their houses which were not only full of racing cars and teepees but also swarming with fathers, mothers, brothers and sisters. The time I spent with them, usually limited to an afternoon, was for me both painful and a relief. To be sure, our first minutes together were always accompanied by a sense of contentment with myself and the world; but as soon as I was confronted with the inevitable end of my visit, a feeling of envy and of being at a disadvantage came over me – less, however, on account of the concrete objects themselves but due to another person's feeling of ownership and to the unproblematic closeness in human relations which the exchange of presents signifies.

Whenever I was at Bernd's house to play, I felt as though life could adjust to my needs, and not the other way around. Had there been chasms none the less, one could have floated across them – that is how much my senses were captivated by something that to him was a normal part of life. Bernd did not give the impression of someone who had earned or created this environment for himself, but of one who had from one day to the next been transplanted into this world. He acted unsure, bored but also euphoric when he found in my tongue-tied inability to express myself a quality that his circumstances had hitherto prevented him from experiencing. Bernd's hair was a living memorial to his mother's wild times. She cut with her own hands what she considered was a genuine Beatles' do. And he also owed it to her that from early on his dripping snub nose had to contend with John Lennon-glasses. Perhaps it was her hope that these glasses added a sky-blue eyeful of intellectualism to the somewhat perplexed expression on his face. His lips were as thin as the bits of information they dispensed – which is to say, words he sometimes had to wrest from his compulsion to stutter with as much determination as a sprinter imposes on his motion machine in order to win by that decisive hundredth of a second. His breathing was a little asthmatic, his body leptosom, which also meant that he was scared to death by any venture that would inevitably make one's heart beat faster and one's throat start wheezing. He had a constant, because justified fear of being injured, beaten up or maneuvered into a situation that would demand of him a decision whose possible consequences might affect a person other than himself (his own status being enough of a calamity anyhow!).

And so he took cover – in every imaginable sense of the phrase – and in the center of his fearfulness and his awakening class-consciousness, of his shyness and bragging, of his material abundance and physical disadvantage waited for us to show up scraping and bowing like courtiers in his playroom. While we again and again went down on our knees before this overwhelming concentration of possessions in one single non-person and sweet-talked him so as to expunge from our voices every last trace of those insults we had hurled at him just the day before.

One crossed through the grocery store Bernd's parent owned, its small supply of goods on the ground floor, and came to a stairway that displayed a blasé attitude of its own, being of a highly smooth reddish-brown color beneath a veil-like sheen of black and ascending to something higher – the living quarters on the second floor. This construction which showed surprisingly few signs of wear and tear had not been insulted with the use either of cold stone or of banal timber from our region. As the grandson of a former pulpwood hauler who himself had come into some forest property I knew something about trees, about their strangely inviting and rejecting aura and of the disquiet the wind carried into them without being able to change their flourishing imperturbability. Mahogany, ebony – the stairway decorated itself with names that graced the villas of the rich and beautiful in the women's magazines my grandmother read. A stairway thus also that made it somehow easier to obey requirements such as "Take off your shoes," which one would have resisted at home – at least as much as possible and after careful consideration of the punishment to be expected.

I took my shoes off and went upstairs. The wall was not white as everywhere else but the color of apricots. The whole ambiance announced how important it was to Bernd's parents to stand out from their neighborhood. The color of the wall as much as Bernd's haircut, the stairway, the piano in their living room and holiday destinations like India, which compelled my grandmother to shake her head. How much energy, how much flair and subtlety they must have expended to pull off this tight-rope walk between keeping themselves separate and fitting in! After all, they were running a grocery store whose customers were farm women for the most part to whom tradition and integration meant everything.

Trying to be different is an expansive gesture. I imagine Bernd's youthful mother and how in her mind, while she is listening to Bob Dylan, she threw her right shoulder into a powerful block and tried to shove everything aside in one single forward thrust; and that life became too much of a challenge for her because she hopelessly overtaxed her strength and came close to being thrown off balance.

Before her ambitions had run full circle and she returned presumably to the point from which she had started, unexpected bird's-eye-view perspectives on the world had opened up for her – a world of which a young woman in some little Austrian town in the early 1960s had been dreaming while boredom and an easily excitable ignorance made her skirts get shorter and her kisses more fervent. Until at last, after graduating from high school, she just couldn't stand it any longer and took off on the pillion seat of a Zündapp motorcycle. Not to mention those days when she was pregnant with the theorems of political science rather than with Bernd's older sibling, or when she and like-minded sisters protested against the patriarchy by symbolically beating down on the Klagenfurt dragon with their picket signs. And who knew that she had come back home for good even before the noise of her children stomping up and down the stairway had irrevocably drowned out the last echoes of the old Zündapp.

As my grandmother lay dying, I went back to

Poppichl to see her one last time. My mother was of the opinion that my year-end report card possessed at least as much curative power as the bottle of holy water my grandmother kept on her night dresser. Lotti, a friend of hers from when she was a girl, used it regularly to embrocade the left side of her body that was as good as dead after her stroke. Sitting in the train compartment, I was looking forward so much to the moment when I could give my grandmother a reason to feel joy that I had tears in my eyes. But I knew at the same time that I would probably not get myself even this time to shove the chamber pot under the bedridden woman's behind and empty it afterward without making her feel that she was dirtying me. She would start weeping, softly at first and then vehemently, but more about her situation than because of me. She would remind me of the many times she had done this chore for me when I was a child. Then she would come around to mentioning that she was nothing but a bother to us and that we should let her die at last. She was serious about it. At one time she went on a hunger strike, day after day swiped the lunch that Social Services provided off its tray and doggedly closed her mouth when they tried to feed her. Not until she was too weak to fight back was the doctor able to inject her with a tranquilizer and to persuade her that she should start eating again.

During the course of my visit I also walked over to see Bernd, but only his parents were home. It was shortly after closing time, and they insisted on my staying for dinner. "The children are all of them gone," their mother told me, and even though I knew that they – with the exception of Heiner who had moved to Berlin – still lived at home in their old rooms, she made it sound as if they had emigrated and had not been heard from ever since. I looked at her briefly from the side. The corner of her mouth, her eyelids, all the laugh-and-worry lines seemed aggrieved all of a sudden and as if burdened with a heavy weight. The pleasure of seeing me again that I believed I had noticed briefly in her face when she first greeted me went down the drain of this sudden upsurge of old age. Later she said: "So you're going to go to college some day." Her husband interrupted his meal that very moment, pressed his lips together and gave me an encouraging look which encapsulated just about everything that must have happened with him from the day he himself had reached the very same decision. So that I was no longer sure for whom this encouragement was really meant: for me or himself.

The impression of a fleeting sense of superiority will always be a very special factor when the endangered, vain ego needs caressing, will be a form of social advancement during a second of fearful disorientation. The eyes of Bernd's parents were glued on me like decals of their thoughts that went along with every movement of my head as it happened. Perhaps they assumed I would finish something they had been forced to give up? Of course, I might fail just as well. But for the length of this one evening, at this table I had arrived at the finish line that had once also been their destination. My mother was fearful that I might deviate from the road to success she believed she had smoothed for me. She hated that propensity for excess, for insubordination in me. Secretly she hoped that I might work off these dangerous tendencies by using girls whom I would discard soon afterward before I returned – free now of these impulses and strengthened – to the task of my advancement in society.

The moment I first stepped across the threshold of Bernd's room as a child, I was confronted with the futility of trying to be only myself and not someone else. But after all, one has dreams of leaving the prison of one's own identity in the belief that it is freedom one finds on the other side and never a new prison: the prison of the others. I could barely believe how different a child's playroom might be. Walls with posters everywhere, tape recorders, a turntable, a bed with Donald Duck sheets. I slept in my grandparents' old bed, in a corner next to the clothespress. When grandfather came home, he would stagger through my room on his way to bed.

Bernd had his walkie-talkies, his baseball outfit, his remote-controlled Porsche, his . . . All I ever had was perhaps my new machine gun which, when I pulled the trigger, would shoot off sparks behind a red plastic disk. But I had Bernd and the isolation into which he had slipped on account of his indecisiveness, whininess and probably also this certain snobbery of his parents. Bernd never joined one of our gangs. He was building a fortress out of Lego blocks while we were constructing a tree house out of boards and branches. He went swimming in their backyard pool that one could cross in one forceful stroke while we took our bicycles and rode out to one of the marsh ponds near Poppichl. He never came to play pinball since he played against himself on his own little pinball machine. And while we were sitting in the driveway behind our house, throwing tennis balls against the barn door or tearing an earthworm apart, he studied the structure of a fly's eye under his microscope.

He always made a slightly frightened impression when I showed up at his house unannounced. But in the final analysis he was grateful that I had come on my own initiative since he would have been much too bashful to ask someone to come to his room. I turned this gratitude to my advantage by making sure to visit him only when his grandmother, and not his mother, was sitting behind the cash register and taking care of the store. Only with her could he muster enough courage to gather the supply of chocolate, cola and chips I demanded.

This could have been the prelude to my unscrupulously taking advantage of him. Whichever toy I came to like – he was immediately willing to let me keep it. He virtually forced me to have it, which again and again sent his mother over to my grandmother's to retrieve what I had in the meantime hidden in my room. The gullibility with which he took everything I told him for gospel truth made him an ideal partner of the braggart others would at once have unmasked me to be. And finally: the light on his forehead that never faded into a ponderous frown. Eyes like open windows in a house of a face: that somebody had come to play with him made the light in his pupils sparkle. And in those days he had not been ashamed to let me know this, or at least had not been able to keep his body from expressing itself in this way. All this made it impossible for me to fleece him badly or tell him a pack of lies.

Friends we became only when we managed to transform a dead bird into a secret that went on living inside us.

We thought at first it was simply a piece of stone. But the thing changed with every step we came closer. Was it not covered with a filmy sheen? Our hope that we had found a meteorite was soon giving way to the probability that his object was something furry, perhaps an animal. Until at last we could tell by its feathers.

The falcon had not, we were sure of that, been struck by lightning in mid-air, or else its brown plumage with its delicate, parchment-white streaks and spots would have been burned, and we would have thought it to be a lump of peat or lignite.

We had gone down on our knees; Bernd was practically kneeling before the creature. Was this perhaps an expression of respect that the presence of death – most of all the death of something beautiful – elicited from us instinctively? When one had encountered it so unexpectedly that there had been no time to think it over and when the creature embodied both being dead and being alive. It was strange: a star seems to have fallen out of the sky and not have burned up. We looked at one another, baffled that there could be an ambivalence about these things when they lay right in front of your feet: being there/not being there, being dead/being alive. Even though it was written that the Resurrection of Jesus had defeated Death, and that we could all, given the appropriate conduct on our part, meet again in Heaven. (My grandmother firmly believed in this, while my grandfather and my mother were of one mind in their conviction that it amounted to nothing but utter nonsense, probably the only thing they could ever agree on).

Could anything, at first sight, be so inviolate and yet be dead? Wouldn't this also have meant being irredeemably given over to putrefaction? Why should a dead falcon's soul go to heaven anyway when the sky had been his domain all along?

There was something casually irrelevant about all this that repelled, incensed us in connection with this magnificent creature. And that united us, or at least brought us closer together than any earlier, seemingly more vivid occasion had done. How often had it been that all of us had used the name of this animal (most of the time along with adjectives like black or brave) to adorn and thus to reward ourselves? Whoever had taken this name was sure of a good head for heights and carried inside him the aspiration to rise as high as towers.

Only after the grave had been dug in our orchard did we realize that we had not bothered looking for a shovel or something with a sharp edge. We had used our bare hands perhaps because we were afraid that looking for it might attract someone's attention. Our effort to be as inconspicuous as possible had made us sneak across our yard with our backs bent and the muscles in our faces twitching with excitement so that it would inevitably appear we had been up to no good.

The soil was soft. It had rained hard the last few days. As we saw the creature lying there in its wet hole, we had the feeling that the falcon was at peace. Bernd and I stood as close together as never before. A little of the incompatibility of our characters had been thrown into the grave as well. Or we had pushed it out with our sweat as we were digging. Something of the smoldering pressure that comes with the unending game of Who-is-down-and-who-is-up. Hierarchies, rituals never really change, even though a few chips had flaked off our social intransigence, the space between being an insider and a pariah had narrowed a little. Yet for a long time after, when I ran into Bernd in the company of other boys, we treated one another as if the incident of the falcon had never happened. I would simply ignore his presence or make fun of him. He would run away or look at me – blinking his eyes, stuttering and paying no attention to what I was saying. Without talking about it later, we knew that we were play-acting. The earth resting on the falcon, in other words, was also hiding a secret and keeping outsiders from looking into our inner lives.

Sweating and Winking

THE FACT THAT MY FOURTH-GRADE TEACHER had recommended me highly for admission to "Gymnasium" had helped my mother persuade herself that I no longer needed a woman to act as my watchdog, and that I could henceforth live with her. She had meanwhile moved to a larger apartment. I was given my own house key. "Just so we understand each other," she said, "this is no license to kill. And it can be revoked." Which meant that every once in a while she unexpectedly came home during her lunch break, took my key away and locked me in all afternoon without giving any reason. "No discussion." I didn't get away with roaming around the neighborhood after school, waiting for the end of her lunch break. Like Fini, she knew my class schedule and called the apartment when I was supposed to be home.

She had a bedroom of her own with a four-poster under a red canopy. I slept on the sofa and was given a desk and a corner with a pile of pillows. It didn't bother me that my mother could, both from the door and from her place at the dinner table, see everything I might be doing there because she was hardly ever at home anyway, which meant I had not just a corner but the whole apartment to myself. When she came home from work, she made herself coffee and we watched one of the early-evening shows together. I would be standing on the balcony waiting, indeed trembling to see her car turn into our street. It was more than important to have her be there on time because only when we watched a movie together from the beginning could it become an event for me that we could share like that secret the male hero was trying to uncover. During this half hour, the missing years in our lives had been spliced together like strips of film.

Afterward she prepared dinner and my lunch for the following day – precooked meals to which I would add the boiled rice or noodles I had learned how to fix without help. On four out of five evenings she then locked herself into the bathroom to change into a woman she was convinced every man would want to take out to a concert or to a restaurant. After that she disappeared in the bedroom and selected the dress or suit appropriate for the occasion. I waited in the living room for her to show off the dresses from which she made her choice. Of course, *my* judgment was less important here than a certain tingling that a piece of clothing aroused on her skin. The door to the bedroom opened. My mother anticipated what was to happen and on the vestibule carpet held a review of those bashful and greedy looks people would throw at her this evening. She walked through the door, came a few steps toward me, pouted her lips and turned round in a circle. "How do I look? How do I look?" she asked. Then she casually walked away and left me with the promise of her waggling behind, a promise that, without being meant for me anyway, at this point transcended the range of my imagination.

After she had made her selection – dress, perfume, jewelry, shoes, underwear, stockings (never pantyhose), purse, powder, eyebrow pencil, eyeliner, lipstick, highlight pencil, nail polish, deodorant –, she took my head in both hands and kissed me on the forehead and the mouth. A string of blond hair slipped between our lips. She had let her hair grow out until it fell down nearly to her hips. When she was looking at herself in the mirror and shook her head, her hair was like a silent wind chime. She went to the door. I sniffed after the cloud of perfume surrounding her. At this moment I missed her as much as I cursed her the very next, when she returned, smiled at me and put the cable to the TV antenna in her handbag.

The key turned, and in locking my door closed off the world behind it. I lay in bed. My life had little importance. It weighed almost as little as a sheet of paper. My bedcover pressed down on me like a paperweight. I didn't know what to do. Comics no longer interested me, and I had rummaged through my mother's dressers and wardrobes several times before, which couldn't possibly have escaped my mother's attention. But apparently it had not bothered her much since everything that was not meant for my eyes had been put away in drawers she always kept locked. At first I had always checked right after she left to see if she had forgotten to lock one of them. But even when she was in the greatest hurry, when we could hear through the open balcony door that one of her admirers was honking his car horn at ever shorter intervals, she wouldn't forget; and finally I gave up. I recognized in the course of time how much it meant to her to let me know that nothing could get her so excited, could so get under her skin that she would get careless over it and not follow through on something until she had finished it.

In my mind I picked up the ball and kicked it at the chandelier which already had lost two of its crystal drops the last time I had, in defiance of my mother's prohibition, played soccer in the apartment. My mother had slapped me in the face for this, but she did not confiscate my ball because she wanted to force me to look temptation in the eye.

I felt better when I imagined the chandelier shedding

glittery tears or my mother's dresses, pants, bags, belts and shoes catching on fire and slowly burning to ashes. I had the feeling that my face was washed in a wave of grins while in my mind I devastated my mother's furniture and clothes. Moreover, I held my penis in my hand. Just a few minutes before, it would have been impossible for me to masturbate. But now my thoughts had breathed new life into my hand, and it moved. My dick grew in it, as did I, until this growing and moving at last brought about thoughts of quite a different kind that liberated me from the prison of my surroundings for good.

The beginning of all masturbation, I think, comes with the child's screams and not with its being suckled. With discontent, and not with a sense of well-being. Screams serve not just to fend off hunger, pain and the first presentiment of solitude and abandonment. Only when it screams out its lungs can a child give itself over to that fundamental masturbatory illusion: to make use of the limited opportunities its own body offers so that it may forget for a few moments the limitations imposed on its own life.

While my grandmother was working in the barn or in the orchard, I was lying within earshot in a crib inside the front door. When the sun was shining, she would bundle me up in a baby buggy and park me under the chestnut tree. Perhaps she thought that looking at a white wall or peeking through the holes between the leaves – which every gust of wind would rearrange and through which the sun was blinking its eye – provided enough vivacity for a while to entertain a creature like me who was on the point of having those experiences which suggest that one can spend one's time either happily or unhappily, left to die or at a woman's bosom. The only way to dispel this misconception was to scream. The time it took was suffocating me. My face turned red as a lobster. Never before had I made such a fuss, and made it with such a show of energy as to give the impression I might climb out of my crib any moment and walk out of the door. I was a magnet. Somebody would have to give in to the irresistible pull of this heart-rending noise. Somebody simply had to come! Had to interrupt her chore, forget her own problems and give me the breast, the bottle, the rattle. Nothing worked. Nothing assuaged me, shut me off. How could it, since nothing less was at stake here than screaming and its inherent power. At some moment, before the increasingly desperate attention of the adults turned into fury or indifference, suddenly and like a gift – quiet, contentment. I had screamed until I had enough of myself.

When, as a child, I was lying in bed by my grandmother's side, I could be confident that the warmth with which her body charged itself under the cover like a battery was being generated not least in order to help me through the following day and ultimately through my whole life. During the course of the night my body posture adjusted to hers. In her embrace I could draw on her feelings and blossom alongside her body like mildew on damp walls. Armed with such affection, I left her house the next day convinced that nothing untoward would ever happen to me and, moreover, that I could, as it were, hang out all my bad manners like laundry on a clothesline. To have grandmother put me in my place right away did not even amount to so much as an irritation but was part of those rituals that firmly attuned me to the rhythm of each new day.

The reason for such happiness, however, arose not so much from the world around me but from the one I discovered within myself, and it was part of the special distinction that the world had obviously discovered in me; in that blue-eyed, rosy god I was when my smile, like a magic wand, touched the somber expression on the faces of other people and made them luminous. At the height of this conjuration, when I was about four, my self-confidence assumed the freedom of π, i. e., of never coming to an end. Fini, however, was unwilling to grant it even the one day of a fly's life. Outside of my biological existence, from whose needs she profited, everything steadfast about me that could not be taken apart by her and then reassembled as she saw fit, was subject to her hatred. She was ready to pounce on each and every new word I brought back to her from school or after a visit with my mother, as she did on all observations that went beyond the ordinary impressions the shortest way home from school could offer. I learned how to answer her with words that were tantamount to uninterrupted silence.

When I was in my room and felt safe, I often caught my hand clutching my dick, even holding on to it for dear life. I was lying on my bed in the fetal position, knowing only too well that the blood on the mattresses had nothing to do with giving birth and that there was no way for me to hide in this apartment unless I crawled into myself. My body took things into its own hands. It had turned reaching for my penis into something natural, like sweating or winking, even though this automatic reaction surprised me every time it happened. I hardly ever masturbated. My fear of getting caught in the act by Fini was by far greater and more concrete than this infantile urge that came over me only sporadically and as if from outside rather than out of me. I played with the idea of peeing in my bed. When I was at school, Fini would rummage through my room. She called it "straightening it out." What might have happened if on such an occasion she had found a turd under my blanket?

But I myself was much too repulsed by my excreta as to actually go through with a plan of this sort.

At Fini's I couldn't do it because I was afraid to be found out. During vacations, when I went in the attic or into the corn fields with Gerald to jerk off, I often couldn't get it up because I was thinking about it too much and was too afraid of failure. A Yugoslav classmate who had had to repeat a grade once gave me a detailed demonstration with the help of a banana of what was involved in the correct procedure of jerking off. Either you put your hand around your thing and moved your foreskin back and forth, or you concentrated on the edge of your glans and let your hand glide back and forth, putting pressure on your thumb and index finger. Even though this was nothing new to me, I was as much impressed by the calm routine he displayed as I was taken with Gerald's impatience when he plopped down on the ground, pulled his stiff dong out, closed his eyes and went at it (always preferring the foreskin method). I, on the other hand, first had to concentrate and work up an erection – which wasn't easy since Gerald's satisfaction captivated me more than my own.

Gerald's semen splashed up in a high arc – full of exuberance, full of arrogance concerning the end that fate would provide for it a second later by making it slap on the ground and slowly dry up. He did not look at me after he had opened his eyes again. He pulled his pants up and took off. I stayed behind, thinking about Gerald's semen and how for a short moment it had hovered above the world of seeds and growth around it, until a little blister had formed on my foreskin and I called it quits.

Whenever I go somewhere on the train these days, the first place I look for after my arrival is the newsstand in the station's bookstore. The moment I stand in front of the rack with the porno magazines looking for big tits and asses, I feel as though a door is opening behind me. A pair of eyes is denouncing me and changing my blood into a milky gruel. My body stiffens and turns flat like a chalkboard on which is written that I – no matter where life may take me – will always be: a jerk-off. The sponge to wipe this off does not exist. There is no need for me to turn around and realize that nobody is standing behind me and pointing a finger at me. Fini is no longer going to come into my room. And she doesn't need to, either, because in a situation like this I voluntarily return to my bunkbed.

I take a magazine from the rack and flip through it. As always, there is this marriage of convenience of what is titillating and what in its banality is repulsive. The one, unfortunately, often blends into the other: a woman, working hard to be authentic and trying to put passion into her face, and a man, using a craftsman's routine as he sticks his dong into the wall of her ass like a dowel. Magazines above all that show a cluster of actors fucking, sucking and licking each other personify less the spirit of free love than that of law and order. This never-changing ritual, during which three men poke holes into a woman who is down on all fours, pushing her toward each other as if, so to speak, they were raising their dongs inside her body like glasses clinking a toast, until at last, in order to prove the factuality of their performance, they squirt their semen all over her. Everything ugly and *triste* that one would like to see banished if not from the earth, then at least from one's own head is lurking in these magazines, again and again turning the scene of one's own desires into a pigsty that needs to be cleaned out periodically.

And then at last the one perfect picture after all, the one to inhale, to take into one's mouth and devour. A black woman is shown lying on her back in a pose of perfect self-satisfaction and throwing at me like a high-gloss meal the raw chicken flesh of her inner labia. The darkling hole they frame represents all the things unsaid and unfulfilled as much as they signify the promise to let me forget for a few minutes everything I had missed. I am of two minds. On the one hand, I am intoxicated; on the other, I'm once again disappointed with myself. I look at myself through the eyes of an outsider who condemns me for what I do and for my compulsive desires. And I join in this condemnation. Because one part of me is that outsider and through me lives every day in the world of those norms and concepts which have made him what he is. I cower like a dog who doesn't know what he is being beaten for.

A Source Runs Dry

THE HALL LIGHT WENT OUT. My father looked intimidated and in need of protection – just like the potted flowers around him that our neighbor had brought in for the winter. He shivered a little. His arms were hanging down as if they were lifeless. The confident smile I had noticed through the peephole in the door had disappeared from his face. In his getup he reminded me of the mailman who would stand before me in his baggy blue uniform and with a ball-point pen in his hand, trying to prop himself up.

Even as a child I did not think of him but of someone else. For example, the hero in a TV-series who, in order to make his way in a hostile world, had to employ unpleasant methods and could not spare any time for his wife and child. ("Well, think again," my mother would say. "In the evening, when he had no money and television bored him, he'd tie one on. Then it was 'off to bed!' If I was lucky, he'd bang me. If I wasn't, he'd hit me. And that stupid young cow that I was accepted all this because I thought that's the way it goes, a man has to be like this, at least a little. In the beginning, when he was still wild and not brutal, I even enjoyed it. But very soon all I could think of was: 'How do I get out of here alive?'")

The man who now was walking down the stairs under my watchful eyes until his hazelnut-brown corduroy jacket had completely vanished in the darkness of the lower floor, the last sign of his existence coming from the metallic snap of the closing entrance door, in a way lived on only in my imagination. He had retreated the way a bashful child withdraws his hand from the grasp of a stranger. A child who was missing his mother's legs behind which to hide and peep out with curiosity. He had reverted to being something other than a man made of flesh and blood, much less a person about whom I could entertain a little more than the bare assumption that an indelible trace of him might be found in the building blocks of my body.

The last time he had said goodbye to me I had trotted after him in the railroad station, trying to force myself on him like a piece of luggage. But he had pushed me aside without having to give me a shove or a reprimand. Baggage was mummified life to him. This piece one had bought in this city, that piece was a present from such and such a woman. The less one carried around, the better. These odds and ends from the passing of time stuck to one's life like the lines on a face. Whoever discarded this stuff and the people connected with it before it was too late, would chomp down on the future as if it were a piece of raw meat. "Only the essentials," he said. Obviously, that didn't include me.

Before he got on the train, he stopped in front of me and looked at me for a long time. I thought I could feel his stare penetrating my eye holes so as to anchor itself in my brain as an imperishable memory for the length of his absence. He didn't want to carry the burden of anyone's background, not even his own, and yet like the specter of a living past – indelible, unexpurgated – he hovered over the lives of other people.

He chewed gum and constantly smoothed down his hair. He whistled always the same melody and sometimes did a little dance, turning round in a circle like that gramophone record with the paean to eternal youth that animated all his gestures. I was horrified by the fact of his hairy chest. His yellow shirt was unbuttoned halfway down, and I imagined him tearing it off his body in a compulsive fit as if it were an accursed appendage and revealing to me the hole in his chest. An emptiness that drove him onward like a black heart.

In part, this and a number of similar perceptions of him arose from the fact that his life and his personality were surrounded by an aura of peril and even criminality that was titillating no less than repulsive. He was the son of well-situated parents, and, instead of breaking with society per se, he scrupulously trampled on the bodies and souls of some of its individual members. As a matter of fact, the most horrific and insane stories about him were making the rounds, as though he had spent his life on the movie screen, or had been swashbuckling through the literatures of different cultures. He himself remained untouchable, being both motor and victim of the speed that kept pushing him and which the train he had just boarded would have to work hard to keep up with. I turned round in time and left before he could lower the compartment window and say goodbye to me. (I should say before he forgot or something else could divert his attention).

From time to time, whenever he felt like it, he popped back into our lives – like a toothache or an unsuspected tax audit. Did he need money? But whether he had money to throw around or needed to borrow some; whether he pulled up driving a Jaguar or whether the condition of his soles rather left you with the impression that for quite a while he hadn't even been able to come up with bus fare; whether the gray veil of his sweat-soaked and crumpled shirt darkened his none the less sparkling smile; whether he was indeed on top of it all or whether his visit gave him the illusion that it represented the alternative to a free fall into a deep abyss: no matter, he never truly came back. Rather, he always tried to act like a monument erected to the role he believed he had played in my mother's life – and failed miserably. I couldn't help remembering the way she had once faced him down. She had rammed her high heels into the shag runner and had also mentally prepared herself to administer a possibly necessary kick. Ostensibly bored stiff by life's sentimental need for dusting off old hats whenever the opportunity arises, she would have been the ideal frame for the picture of himself he had shown to me out in the hallway.

When I made a call to my mother in the office to inform her of his sudden return, she laughed this laughter of hers that always gave me the feeling that she had been watching all this from a secret place and had already rendered her verdict. When she came home in the evening, I joined her in the kitchen. Her silence drowned out the puffing gurgles of the coffee maker. She lit a cigarette. "He has been a vagabond all his life," she said without looking at me. "Always just passing through. The devil only knows where all he's been knocking around. And it had to be the day when I split up with my old boyfriend – that just had to be the day he shows up in our village. As if there had been no other place for him in the whole world than our shit pile of a town. At the local whoop-de-doo I wanted to put it to Adi – he was my boyfriend at the time, Adolf Prilassnig, or what you might call a boyfriend, considering that we both didn't know a thing about anything – I wanted to get back at Adi. That's when he suddenly stood there right in front of me. Boy, was he a dancer, your progenitor, one has to grant him that. I was literally floating across the dance floor, not even that moronic oompah-pah-pah-music would bother me any longer. We all liked American music so much better. Well, anyway, what happened is I gathered up my things, and that same night I took off. Like in the movies, 'cause there was nothing to keep me, 'cause I had nothing I could have given up. I left a letter for my mother telling her not to worry, it would be better for all of us and I'd get in touch with her, etc. I thought we were companions, he and I. Each adding that part the other had been lacking until now. So, what do you expect? I too read those little romance novels that were popular at that time, what else was there? The only television set far and wide was to be found in the tavern your grandfather considered his real living room. Talk about companions!"

She laughed again. A teary-eyed hoarseness was rubbing against her vocal cords. "Like a dog he treated me that people abandon when they leave for their vacation. More than once he left me behind in whatever dump, simply locked away, and he didn't come back until it suited his fancy. I had nothing to eat, no kitchen stove, no electricity, telephone. Or he would . . ." She made a croaking sound, her voice rising with the fire in her that was never quite extinguished. " . . . try to turn me into cash when he needed money. Or just cigarettes. Anyone who paid enough could have me. I felt like I was on the cattle market."

Is it sarcastic of me to assert that there are moments of terrible significance that I owe to my father. When I was a child, my mother and my grandmother had impressed it on me to beware of men I didn't know. Because these strangers – and that was the big difference in similar-sounding reminders other parents would give their children – these strangers might be my father. I had memorized – just as I had the alphabet, which it was impossible not to keep in mind if one wanted to get ahead step by step in a world that was like a staircase – had internalized the rules of conduct my mother had devised for use in an emergency. And when one day during my summer vacation he did in fact show up on my grandparents' farm and, a box of chocolates in his hand, declared himself to be what my mother, leaving all biologically incontestable evidence aside, had forbidden him ever to claim, I transformed myself into the escape apparatus that had been constructed for this very purpose. I immediately turned around, ran across the yard into the house and several times hollered like crazy: "Gran'ma, gran'pa, dad is here!" Then I ran up the stairs into the bedroom and hid under the bed where my grandmother's emptied chamber pot kept me company. From there I could listen in as my grandmother ordered my father to stay away from this house. "Get lost!" she hurled at him like a triple sign of the cross. "Get lost! Get lost!" she hollered again, only with more furious, more breathless vehemence. "But mama, he's my little boy too . . .", my father replied in a strangely subdued voice. Perhaps he had been taken by surprise to see how hatred and fear were distorting the face of his warm-hearted ex-mother-in-law. Then I heard steps and sounds as when a tape is being played too fast at one moment and too slowly the next. Shortly thereafter a high-pitched and a dark slapping. I imagined her hitting him in the face and against the chest. "But mama! But mama!" he wailed. And into a sudden but for me torturously long silence the screaming voice of my grandmother: "Don't you ever show your face here again, you dog, you!" Then I heard a door being slammed shut and a car driving off. Grandmother was shaking over her whole body when she got me out from under the bed.

After the first time he had stood in front of me and I had heard his voice, my father no longer was a chapter in a book I could either open or leave aside just as I pleased.

He could simply wait until recess, take me by the hand and so make me realize that a part of my future, of my lifetime would from now on also belong to him. I know that for a time my mother was greatly afraid of such a turn in our life, even if or precisely because she did not say much whenever this was being talked about, and she remained weary of a world that did not forever make a piece of garbage, dirt, scum like my father disappear in one of its bottomless chasms.

I don't know when and, above all, in which way we became used to his visits. Not, that we could anticipate them. They were much too infrequent for that. But this absence of any bit of subsequent change, this stunted repertoire of words and gestures, of human interchanges, let my mother see an insecurity in her ex-husband that she had not expected and which, though it didn't necessarily confirm her side of the story, helped to strengthen her position. If he had come over me like a flash of lightning or like a power outage or at least had come to our door triumphantly showing a court order . . . Instead, the older I was getting, the more my father and I faced one another like two pubescent males: a man, a boy, shy glances, nervous stepping-in-place, fingernail-biting. And always the same questions, for which I had no words but only a nod or a shrug of the shoulders: had I forgotten who he was? how was I doing in school? what was she telling me about him? and that some day he would explain it all to me. And then he would give me a little money and a soccer ball or new sneakers which invariably were too large or too small.

There came a time when I had indeed as good as forgotten him. Since his visits lacked continuity, he could not, even had he wanted to, become something predictable in my life. I didn't, to be honest, want to have a father, but a family like all other children. That there were other children of divorce, who more or less had to do without one half of their parents, was immaterial to me. What counted in my eyes were only those fervently envied individuals who had what I imagined to be a perfect family. Father. Mother. Siblings. In a certain sense, though, I even had several fathers – certainly the highest number of them in comparison with my classmates. Almost all men my mother brought home wanted to be something like a father to me for the length of a breakfast together, or a turbulent month, or an unexpected relationship. Their calculating men's hands approached me the way one approaches a dog that is no longer just a puppy: with caution but resolutely – hoping that the caresses and intimate pats on the boy's head would succeed all the better with his mother's lips, breasts and vagina.

The wishes and aims of these men provided an ideal forum for the sort of presumption and impudence that would never have entered my mind in the presence of other adults. Indifference, haughtiness, overstepping the limits of their authority in our apartment were subject to immediate punishment. Depending on my age, I turned prudish, rebellious, lachrymose, aggressive, doing everything in my power to make my mother feel that my behavior was to be attributed exclusively to a lack of sensitivity on the part of our visitor.

But it did not happen too often that I needed to resort to such devices. On the one hand, because I was allowed only on a few occasions anyway to stay overnight with my mother before I was old enough for "Gymnasium"; on the other, because my mother's admirers were attorneys, architects, trust fund administrators – men who first and foremost paid attention to the laws of predictable behavior, to the logic of investment and return. They came prepared. They inspected me. They could tell in no time that I was corruptible. I didn't even try to hide this – on the contrary. It may sound strange but for me the decisive factor about my mother's male acquaintances was always the armpit area, that part of their physique between ribcage, elbow and axilla into which they had wedged something they would give me in order to curry favor with me (for example, a new race track). They had to pay for the fact that they and not I were allowed to sleep in my mother's bed. They were hunters, I had turned into a gatherer. There was probably no better way we could complement each other. But I was only the ticket-taker. I had no power to change a script that staged the real performance in my mother's bedroom.

The few of them who wanted to marry my mother met with disappointment. She didn't want to get married again. When she heard any man pursue this as a possibility, the lines under her make-up would tighten to form a mask that looked deceptively like her face and into which she could retreat abruptly and, they thought, for no apparent reason. She didn't want one more ugly ink spot in the book of her life. Being both its narrator and heroine, she kept as firm a grip on her story as she possibly could. She was at least as much afraid of the happiness that takes away one's breath as she was scared of the misery that would happen faster than people could react.

The danger of being taken out of my context like a single sentence out of a speech had been averted. Or, as my mother put it: "In the end, life's reckoning did catch up with him!" Had he extended his hand to me out there in the hall and if I could have made myself reach for it – what might have happened? Would he have tried to squeeze me into his life as into an old suit I had meanwhile outgrown by two sizes? Why had he made not the slightest effort at least to get into the apartment? Had he not expected to encounter the kind of person he did find there and who may have differed from the one he had kept in his fading memory? Was that the reason he could barely muster the will to look him in the face?

I would not, in any case, have put my hand into the palm of his mute greeting if I could help it. I didn't want to be caught in an embarrassing situation. I knew there was no logical reason for me to feel charitable toward the wretched figure my father had become. I had no reason to wish the plague on him, as my mother did. I simply found it unfair that obviously he had – or so I believed – withheld his good years from me and now was trying to let me share his bad ones. (If I hadn't at that time thought about nothing but what I had missed, I might have recognized that through his absence he had in fact saved me from his bad years and their insignia – unpredictability, violence, stupefaction and a painful awakening with thirst for revenge; that he had become a person whose body had ceased being his ally and whose energy had been used up by the aimless excesses of his lifestyle; who wanted to make his peace with himself and with me, but didn't quite know how).

The shadowy specter had disappeared again from my life. The blackness of years past had swallowed him once again.

A long time later my father was standing at the entrance door of the café where we had agreed to meet. For a moment his body delimited the turmoil of the street: pedestrians, cars, a well-stocked row of houses wrapped into a gray foil of exhaust fumes. Other guests were pushing past him in and out of the door. He walked over to a clothes tree, took his overcoat off and for a long time let his eyes wander across tables and guests. Only when he looked in my direction for a second time and I met his eyes straight on did he recognize me. Even before he shook my hand, he asked me where the restroom might be. I was nonplused to realize how he – whether intentionally or unawares – would manage again and again to be present and yet beyond reach. After he returned from the bathroom, he hardly spoke a word. He downplayed the illness he had mentioned to me on the phone in a few brief sentences as if it were nothing but an annoying visitor who would soon leave again. I was sitting across from a stranger who had assumed a role in my life by having begotten me. That he was to die soon, made me feel affectionate toward him for a moment. At the same time, I was curious to find out what the closeness of death might persuade him to do or say. Would there be confessions or acts of restitution? Why else would he have called me up in the middle of the night to ask me if we could meet somewhere? Perhaps he did want to keep what he had always promised me when I was a child and explain everything.

After a half hour which we had spent more in silence than in conversation he suddenly felt hungry. He tried to invite me out to dinner, which I politely declined. I was surprised by the hearty appetite with which this seriously ill man attacked his goulash. During this whole procedure of biting into it, of chewing, drinking and being silent he held a cloth handkerchief in his left hand, squeezing his fingers into a firm grip around it. Did he need to hold on to something? Or had he tied it into knots to help him remember things?

As if he had guessed my thoughts, his eyes rested on me with pale-gray irony. Age dims one's eyesight but not always one's gaze. I faced his and was surprised to find in it not myself but my grandfather.

"Isn't all of that just so much insanity?" my father asked more himself than me. When he put his left hand plus handkerchief on my right lower arm and his eyes, moist with tears, lit up in the slanting rays of the sun, I knew what he wanted to leave me: an image of himself as a different, better person.

Taking Off and Falling Down

I KICKED THE SMALL, soft plastic ball past the boy, who lived in the same house as I, into the goal. The ball slammed against the concrete wall. The concrete muffled the noise so that none of the tenants complained when we played soccer in the driveway in front of the garages. Aside from the dull thud of the ball and the scuffling of our rubber soles, there was only the occasional triumphant shout after a spectacular goal that found its way across the sidelines of our play enclosure, which opened out into the street and was painted in bad-weather colors. Our piercing yells, though, did not rise high enough to make somebody on the second floor close his window or shout back an unfriendly reaction. The quietness of our way of playing, characterized as it was by panting and sweating and a constant flailing of the arms, was due not the least to the firm rules we had agreed on that enjoined us from fighting for the ball and from its inevitable accompaniment of ferocious screams about which the tenants would have complained to the super immediately. One of us guarded the goal, the other tried to kick a goal without being allowed to advance on the goal beyond a certain point.

The game that emerged from such a constellation was less a game against a flesh-and-blood opponent than against inert matter – against the unwieldiness of plastic and the inflexibility of concrete. Never again did I hear the factory music of my tendons and muscle fibers, of my bones and cartilages more clearly then during the silent-film-like hectic of this struggle to score goals. Even though the asphalt surface was level, one would trip up again and again and lose one's footing as if the ground were overgrown with roots that had pushed through it. The ball, in turn, would plop off the wall if one didn't boot it with the requisite determination and would stick to the ground like an apple that had dropped off a tree. This interplay of kicking and buckling, of stretching and overextending made me feel and, yes, hear the raw mechanism of my body at work. The whole labor force of my motion apparatus went to the limits of what can reasonably be expected. There was grinding and pinching, pulling and tearing close to the point of snapping; there were spills with quick dislocations and equally quick readjustments of the anatomical arrangement. It was a source of happiness for me to experience how the factory of my body, how the instruments of its various departments were cooperating so that they were able to execute the orders coming from my brain. And then I realized that I was strong and in possession of a physical robustness that had been unknown to me before.

My mother bought me blue iron barbells weighing over ten pounds. I stood up against the wall, leaning my back against it and with my legs apart. I pressed the barbells from my upper legs to the height of my chest and then let them sink back onto my legs, holding the tension in my tendons and muscles. I overdid it to the point where my arms felt like they had been changed to the consistency of dried glue and I had to drop the barbells on the floor, which thanks to the carpet left no dents on the hardwood floor underneath. Although I had until then displayed little inclination to excel at sports, my mother showed as little surprise about all this as she did about my decision to join an athletic club. Sports, after all, was something obvious and close at hand: it started with one's own body at rest and ended with one's own body accelerated or weighed down.

I imagined myself moving forward, my body expanding and myself changing in the process and morphing into someone who could no longer be overlooked quite so easily in class as during the first two grades. I had been a very good student in elementary school. In "Gymnasium" my grades had been no less average than the interest I had evoked among my classmates. Many of them had attended the elementary school nearby. I wanted to be accepted into their circle. I looked for something within or about me that they might find worth owning or striving for, and I discovered nothing but the possibilities my body offered me. I did not want to be among the outsiders in our grade – a number of lost monads circling around themselves and whose absence no one would have noticed if the teacher had not been required to record this fact on the attendance roster at the beginning of class.

I was presumptuous enough to think that I owed it to my muscles and the fine figure I suddenly cut and not to my unexpected abilities in Latin, when classmates suddenly invited me to their houses after they had paid almost no attention to me for nearly two years.

Sometimes I did not go home right after school but headed directly for the sports field. The coach for my age group was not on the premises before 4 p.m. He was very close to retirement and had a twirled mustache the tips of which pointed upward and away from his upper lips as stiffly as the horn-rimmed glasses on the bridge of his nose. It was his ambition to make, if not European champions, then more useful citizens of us than, in his opinion, we were now. He promised that we would get to know him and afterward would no longer remember who we were. Also not, what we excreted, our sleep and television habits, masturbation and girls. In the manner of a preacher he demanded that we renounce the habits of our conduct because they were mentally and physically unhealthy. In personal conversations he tried to make us believe that we had been chosen for something extraordinary. We were not supposed to speak of this with anyone and not let anything about it slip out during practice. This would only bring about little jealousies that would be an impediment on the road to the Olympics. Whoever could not agree that sports is a form of contest and that one contestant always wanted to triumph over the other, might as well pack up right away. A team was an essential, but a purely functional construct. The passing of the baton during a relay race did not express the need to reach out to the other runner's hand but the will both to extend one's own hand to the other's body and to push one's own will into him.

In those days, when I paced off the length of the track that circled the soccer field like a wide, black-grained zero, there was nobody on the grounds but me. The asphalt circle of the shot-putters, the nylon net of the discus throwers – everything had been dropped in place with the gesture of an ultimatum as if this were the New Year's Eve custom of telling the future by pouring molten lead into water. Not even the attendant could disturb this still life by shoveling sand into the broad-jump pit or by using a sponge to remove the puddle of water that always collected on the long-jump mat.

I put my running shoes on. They were two sizes smaller than regular shoes so that they fit my feet like a second layer of skin. There was to be no difference between the sole in my shoe and that of my feet if I was to hit the track and snap back like a hammer on metal. At the very same instant that the naps under the shoes dug into the track's cinders, they had to lift off the ground. As a sprinter I had to race toward the finish line with the undistractible immediacy of a bullet fired from a pistol – as if the air were kicking against my body so long as it was at rest, leaving it in peace only during its forward motion.

Two options were open to javelin throwers. Either, one became domesticated in the power room and force-fed his body with power food until it resembled a bulk of freezer meat, packaged airtight, that was able to throw the javelin over 200 feet when told to and using not more of an effort than a punch needs to put two holes into a piece of paper. Or, one tried to fathom the imponderabilities of the javelin and its aerial arc, which drove even experienced athletes close to despair when at the decisive moment of the competition one of the throws would all of a sudden be fifteen feet longer or thirty feet shorter even though every aspect of the throw had been executed exactly as the preceding ones. Anybody who had been wrestling with the idiosyncrasies of the implement for some time would swear that it was not just a matter of the personal shape one was in, or of the unsettled wind conditions. Rather, the javelin had a life of its own that one could never get under control one hundred per cent. Whoever may want the breezes to become his ally and the javelin to go on working for him, as it were, while it was in flight, would have to send it on its way with the same kind of unthinking naturalness with which he butters his bread in the morning.

For almost a year I tried to put the occasionally cryptic instructions passed on by this philosophical section of the club to good use. It was hopeless. As easy as it was for me after some time to display my biceps, triceps or latex in the schoolyard or on the bus without making it obvious, so impossible was it for me to repeat a successful throw on the same day even once. I was bored stiff in a short time to be thinking about a javelin and why after a throw it would wobble through the air like a punctured balloon, or why it took off like a firecracker. Consequently, going out to practice contributed less to my knowledge of the implement than it did to my realization of how serious I truly was about sports and what I hoped to gain from an almost daily commitment to keep practicing – to tell the truth, not more than to cut a good figure in my gym class, in the swimming pool and in front of girls.

After I came home from work-outs, I didn't hurry to do my homework but sat down in front of the hi-fi-tower. The cabinets for the radio, amplifier and cassette deck had a silver sheen and were stacked one on top of the other inside a construction of chrome-colored rods and stays. Add the record player that surmounted it and this whole arrangement came up to my chest. The chrome, the metal, the Plexiglas front of the radio receiver – the arrangement was like a mirror that reflected one's own facial features, sometimes blurred and then again sharply defined, or made them appear in a soft light. I don't know what captivated me more: putting an LP and the headphones on and listening to the music with my eyes closed, or sitting face to face across from this out-of-focus, unfinished version of myself with which I identified more than with the distinct, un-shakable one looking at me from the mirror in our vestibule. Checking myself on the surface of the music arrangement, I also did not pay special attention to my muscles whose growth I would otherwise register with the same punctilious vigilance that somebody else might devote to the irreversible loss of his hair. It was my eyes that I was looking for and that kept finding me every time. My gaze revealed what I knew anyway: that the granitic self-assuredness emanating from my broad chest had feet of clay and had been eroded by images and dreams of which the music entering me through my auditory canal was alternatively providing the background and the cause. But to close the gap left by an uncertain future in my dreams about who I was going to be, nothing more was needed than the first chord of an electric guitar solo, and I knew in a split second that I had years left during which to have a good time or play fast and loose until, as my mother would say, it was "nose to the grindstone" for me.

Then I went into the room that until recently had been my mother's bedroom and now was to be mine. Everything in this room smelled of her, every piece she left behind – drapes, lamp, carpet – told stories about her so that for a long time I felt like an intruder in my own room. When I walked around the room naked, I sometimes felt as though I wasn't moving about in the air surrounding me but in the vapors of her past.

The day on which I was given my room was also the day on which my mother gave up her canopied four-poster. Even though this had been my wish for a long time, it would never have occurred to me to ask her if we couldn't exchange rooms – that's how unthinkable it was to have my mother end up spending her nights and weekends on the lumpy pull-out bed in our living room. Her disco-crawls ended like the glass of champagne she was emptying before my eyes in one gulp as she danced on the table – she tossed it behind herself full of verve and couldn't care less where it hit or whether the pieces of broken glass would cause any damage. I could hear the same kind of clatter when her lovers would invariably run into the umbrella stand in our vestibule at two in the morning and sometimes even knock their heads against the shoe chest, which made my mother laugh so uproariously that I was sure she had placed the stand there on purpose. By then I was fully awake and could hear her laughter change the drunken moans of their nocturnal carousing into a furious snarl which segued into a bark promising that he would "you just wait a minute" show her what is what. My mother probably made his blood boil by rattling him with an almost nonchalant air of superiority. "Well, it's about that time now" or "One shouldn't make promises that one can't keep," she would say. I understood close to every word which wasn't ground up between four lips or wasn't pressed onto a neck. And then it wouldn't be long before I heard the metallic squeaking of the mattress springs. Sometimes it was only for seconds, sometimes it seemed there was going to be no end to it.

A week before my mother had furniture movers take her four-poster away, the series of similar incidents, as good as unbroken over the course of years, appeared to be interrupted. Although she didn't dare calling the thing by its name, it seemed that she had fallen in love. Whenever she did not go out with her new acquaintance, she stayed at home in the evening, watched television or went to bed early. Several times I had to deny her presence at home when the crowd, with whom she would normally flit from one bar to the next, called for her on the phone. With this first real friend she ever had for as long as I can remember, she did not go to a disco on the weekend but into the woods. That was the first time I saw her wearing hiking boots – she who for years had driven the cows to their winter pastures and taken lunches to the lumberjacks, wearing hiking boots. The pain in her face from the big blisters on her heels mingled with a pleasure, never experienced before, about something so simple and yet so difficult to attain and which until then she had treated with nothing but ridicule. She bought the first cookbook of her life and put it not on a kitchen shelf but on her little night dresser. Principles hitherto chiseled in stone were bathed in the waves of a smile that would not recede from her lips until they became unrecognizable. During this one "month of her life," as she once called this time years later, I never stood face to face with the cause of these changes more than three, four times. There was not a thing in his neither limp nor firm handshake, in his faraway look and in his tone-on-tone suits that could have provided a clue about why it was him of all people with whom she obviously wanted to give it a second try.

One day I was coming home from javelin practice and wanted to take a shower. My mother was sitting in the bathtub, with the water barely reaching above her ankles and the cheeks of her behind. She had been complaining the last two days about some itching in her pubic area. She said it was getting worse and worse and that she was likely to scratch herself raw. She was thinking of a fungus. The green caustic solution in which she was sitting now was a disinfectant bath which the doctor she had gone to see during her lunch break had prescribed.

From the kitchen I could hear my mother stepping out of the tub and draining the water. I turned the radio on and waited for her to come out of the bathroom. She didn't. "How long is it going to take you?" I shouted. There was no answer. At last I rapped against the bathroom door and opened it when there was no answer again. She was squatting on the floor. She had put her red bathrobe on and was smoking a cigarette, flicking its ashes on the blue floor tiles. With her left hand she clasped the aluminum chain with the bathtub plug. "Is it something bad?" I asked. Without looking at me, she extinguished her cigarette on the floor and turned around. She knelt down and bent over into the bathtub. I could hear her long fingernail scrape across the enameled bottom of the tub. Then she straightened herself out and turned around to face me. She cautiously extended her right index finger toward me holding the palm of her hand up. I bent down. Not until my nose was about to touch the tip of her finger did I see the little dot under her fingernail. "Crab lice," she said. "They are transmitted during sexual intercourse. The doctor could tell right away." Her friend had returned from a business trip three days before.

It ended without a big scene, without wailing or screaming fits. "Ah, you know," she said to me, "I have shed all my tears a long time ago."

As time went by, she more and more spoke about this as if it were an experience she had had with no one but herself – as if a malevolent fate had forced her to spend her life in exile, and as if this one month let her know what a happy feeling it would have been for her to be at home with herself.

During the time after this she often got drunk in the evening which she spent by herself in the living room listening to music. But not to the records that had helped set the rhythm of the four weeks she had spent with him, but records she had not played for years and that had been part of her first months in Salzburg. In the morning it took me no time at all to notice if she had been too drunk to fix her bed and had slept in her clothes. Every now and then she would end up at night in her former bedroom. She would stagger about in the room and bump against the furniture until I turned the light on. She was always surprised to see me. One time she ran at me, screaming what a pig like me was still doing here. Her glassy, slightly bloodshot eyes made her face look as if its picture had been taken with a flash. At last she recognized me and lay down on my bed with her clothes on. I was naked. I wrapped my blanket around me and turned toward the wall. My mother put her arm around me and pressed her body against mine. She was breathing heavily against the back of my head, which created a warm and moist spot. She reeked of alcohol, perfume and hopelessness.

This was no longer the woman of just two years ago whose naked body she let me spray with water from a squirt bottle the way I was allowed to do only with the flowers out on the window sill. She was lying on her back taking a sun bath, two slices of cucumber resting on her closed eyelids. Her nipples were pricking up and she got goose pimples when the silky spray dropped down on her. Sweat, sun oil and water formed small trickles that were searching for her navel as a catch basin to form a little puddle. At first the water got caught on her pubic hair like drops of dew. Then her hair bristled up and stuck together in tufts like the wet pages of a book and afforded me a clear view of her crotch and her labia. Afterwards I went to the toilet and masturbated.

Those days the reddish gleam of my mother's nakedness had excited and disgusted me and had pursued me in my dreams the way that looking at a dog's erection had. This time her bosom and her ribs were pressing against my back, her knee caps against my thighs, and I thought I could sense the impending decay of all this. Of the red flesh only the pallid bones would be left. An apathy that made her eyes dull, her joints stiff and her tongue heavy had taken possession of her and would spread throughout her body until the very last little air bubble of life had risen out of her and she had ceased breathing. In her embrace I was like a fish stranded on a rock and about to be devoured by it and turned into a stone of its own kind. Blood of her blood was turning to stone of my stone.

I gathered all my courage and rammed my elbow into her ribs. First I heard a broken croaking, then a soft whimpering. "*You'll* stay with me, won't you?" she said. "*You'll* stay with me."

Slaps

SHE STRUCK ME FOUR TIMES. So rapidly that I was perplexed, when I thought about it later, where she could take the time for three more slaps after the first one slammed into my face. They made my left cheek ring and, as a kind of echo, produced a whistling in my left ear that stayed on for days and kept me from sleeping at night. "What, if something had happened to you? The insurance wouldn't have paid a schilling."

I had a strange feeling about the whole thing from the start. My mother knew that Herwig, even though he was only seventeen and did not have a driver's license, would sometimes go on joy rides in his parents' second car. She also knew that this afternoon he would drive up again in his ivory-colored and souped-up Vespa, wearing a suit and ready to pick me up. Herwig was two years older than I. After kindergarten he had gone to preschool for a year and had to repeat one grade. It had a liberating effect on me when he, pompous as he was, accepted full responsibility in advance for whatever may happen in the course of our ventures. When we were by ourselves – which did not happen frequently since at that time we hardly had any interests other than running away, meeting girls and getting drunk – the differences in age and experience between us were of no importance. These were occasions when one could recognize a bit in him of the boy his mother simply did not want to associate with the many complaints registered by his teachers. In the presence of others, however, he rarely missed an opportunity to pretend that he felt a little embarrassed to have me along again and that our friendship in fact amounted to the benevolent concourse of a master with a disciple. Our friendship, consequently, was not of long duration.

Why then did my mother not take the keys to her new car with her when she left on a weekend trip with a man she had met? Why did she leave them on the living room table instead, completely contrary to her usual practice? The four slaps in my face left these questions unanswered, being, when taken by themselves, nothing but a string of graphic symbols, empty spaces and punctuation marks that could be tied into the fabric of the whole truth only if you knew their apparent and secret meaning. Her slaps were like an evil curse that someone had furiously sprayed on the wall of a house. My mother's face, illumined by an impassioned, cold fire when she hit me, was the face of a scribe who from one moment to the next abandons the text he is trying to decipher when he realizes that he has wasted years of his life in stuffy, darkened rooms and with the people frequenting them. Her reproaches did not get through to me. They spoke of the outrageous thing that had happened today and of the evil consequences it could have given rise to. Her face, however, in which revenge and retribution made her wrinkled skin grow into a bulge and then flatten out again, spoke of the weeks just past during which she had to witness how my friendship with Herwig had changed me and, as she once put it years later, had estranged me from her. The first time she confronted Herwig, I saw that she found him more than just unpleasant – something I had anticipated and which was perhaps one of my reasons for searching him out in the first place. He had a condescending way about him toward everyone. But she could only perceive it as directed specifically against her and no one else. When she saw him, her eyes were like a personnel file in which every detail was being collected that would at some later time be thrown at me, not him. When they passed one another in the street, he would, instead of greeting her, light a cigarette simply because he felt like provoking her, or for no reason whatsoever. When she was on the kitchen phone, he would be out in the vestibule with me and laugh out loud about the bullshit stories he was telling. When she had gone out in the evening and we were having a little party in my room, he would go through her steady supply of champagne after we had run out of things to drink. Instead of keeping him from going on with this, I would feel pleased about it even when my mother reduced my allowance over an extended period of time. He got me to confront her with the observation that she, as the woman in my life, was a phase-out model, and he did this by baiting me with remarks like "at your age I had taken lots of girls to my room," until I followed his example. I can above all remember the colors of the girl who was the first one to sleep in my bed, without, however, us going all the way. The dress that was rustling and flapping about her was of a washed-out blue that looked like a spring day with a sky whose clouds were all gathering before the sun. Her skin, and her whole personality, felt white and fleeting like the layer of confectioner's sugar on a cake even though the alcohol had made her look tired and heavy. When my mother bumped into us in the hall, I was surprised by her reaction. She didn't leave the impression that she would just as soon have ripped the picture the girl and I had presented into a thousand pieces. Rather, I had the feeling that she was making an effort, though it took some willpower, to accept what couldn't be prevented in the long run anyway. But perhaps I may simply have been too drunk and too intoxicated with my own audacity to be able to recognize that she had done nothing more than decide that she could wait until her time had come.

My feeling that the slaps in my face were a single strike which had been divided into and dealt out in four sections corresponded with the fact that they were both a protest against a severe transgression of the unwritten laws governing life in our apartment, and a demonstration of what measures were at her disposal if I should go on like this. My cheek was burning, there was a whistling in my ear. For a few seconds I had a fuzzy conception of the world and of the situation in which I found myself. For the length of the time it takes the tip of a match to burst into flame on the emery strip of its box, I felt that I was in a position to hit back. But then I was ready to accept that the external circumstances vindicated her: if we had been involved in an accident, we would have been at fault, and she would have been liable to pay for the damages.

But even so, it wasn't on account of her champagne that he drank, of her new car that he drove without a license, or simply of his impertinence, that she had developed such an animus against him. From the top of his head to the bottom of his feet, he truly was what she wanted to be seen as and for this reason had to outfit her body every day with silk blouses, jewelry and fur jackets – a member of high society. His father was an executive of the Salzburg Festival, his mother, a formerly well-known opera singer who had been forced to end her career prematurely for reasons of health. In Herwig my mother recognized the same affectation with which she held a champagne glass or even just a coffee cup; the way she would, with an expense of noise and ceremony, fiddle with a handkerchief or a scarf; the way she would wedge a cigarette between her first two fingers and hold it away from herself so that one might suspect she was flashing someone a V-for-victory sign – or perhaps two ass's ears a child is pinning to the back of another child's head. Whereas my mother, whenever she tried to hide the poverty and restrictions of her childhood from herself and from others and to present herself as something better, always seemed to me like a simple T-shirt with the Chanel trademark imprinted on it, Herwig could command a whole flora and fauna of gestures, mimicry and movements that had been growing out of the soil of his class for generations.

"That all?" I asked to dispel the calm after the fourth slap in my face. My mother shook her head at such a blockhead response and said that she was putting a stop for a while to my going out and "taking little tarts to my room." Secretly I decided even so to continue doing what I had started with Herwig, but to avoid anything that might give my mother an excuse for another explosion like this one.

Vacation

JUST IN TIME, before my skin came off like the peel on a boiled potato, did I pull back my left hand, the red bars of the baking tin blossoming on my fingers. The fine-meshed white squares they created reminded me of the snowflakes that had pierced the sky last night like white bullets.

The section chief shook his head. His eyes revealed the calculations he was running through: how many days of sick-leave I would get, how much money the company had to pay me without getting any work out of me in return. "That same old shit with the winter interns," he said.

The section chief would succumb to an extended sweaty silence whenever he had finished his weekly inspection tour, i. e., had compared the current sales figures with those of the preceding weeks, had checked our compliance with the prescribed distribution of bread, cheese and lunch-meat products in their respective display cases, had scrutinized the cleanliness of the machines and once more had emphasized the requirement of hygienic gloves. None of us felt any obligation to call him back into the reality of the luncheon-meat slicing machine. The employees used hypocrisy and equanimity to protect themselves against a know-it-all attitude that was the result of his trimonthly in-service seminars. How else could friendships have been sustained in the face of his demand, coupled with the prospect of career advancement, that one should always work to outdo others and point out mistakes without mercy? Even though he had sat at the same table with us during lunch break and had stared at every one of us with quickly shifting glances, his words didn't get through to anybody but got lost in a fog of beer and cigarette smoke before they crashed and disintegrated on the table.

While he neatly placed the filled-out checklists in his briefcase, he described for us the special features of his new sports car. His work was done. He had to get on without unnecessary delays to the next branch store. The aura of his authority was gone.

Cold tap water was running over my hand. The hectic response my burns had elicited from the emergency doctor might have suggested that my fingers were in bad shape. I, however, didn't even know if I was still feeling any pain at all or if the pain had become so great that it could no longer be located in one particular part of my body. So that there was no place left – no pore, no joint, no emotion – that was not distorted by pain and thus indistinguishable from pain.

Aside from that, I had every reason to rejoice. The section chief was right: I would not have to work for a while. Which meant for me, who was working during Christmas vacation, that I was free – so unexpectedly free that I thought for a moment that I was free of everything.

There hadn't been any need for me to work during Christmas vacation in the first place. My mother bought me expensive brand-name clothes, a tennis outfit, a portable TV set – but she gave me hardly any money to go out with my friends. She knew that I would rather spend my evenings in front of the TV or reading than be known as the one with the smallest allowance – the fact of my presence at home being more important to her than the chance of having a conversation with me. Often on evenings like these we would be watching the same programs – in separate rooms. I had come to look at the living room as my mother's room. I spent time there only when we had company or when she was not home.

She had started preparing for me the dishes from her cookbook that she had originally wanted to fix for her friend. At first she didn't know what to do with her arms, with the pots and pans, when to add nutmeg, cayenne pepper, oregano. When she kept rotating around her own axis in our tight kitchen, she was like a spinning top that would inevitably spin out of control when it had reached a certain speed. When she noticed that I was watching her out of the twilight in our vestibule, she would stop and stare at me, distorting her mouth in very slow motion and baring her teeth, thereby shedding a pale light like old porcelain, against the background of a long-drawn-out sound emanating from the noman's land between her throat and her chest. She did cook for me, yes, but to witness her struggling with the kitchen utensils and the ingredients, *that* I was not permitted to do.

It had not been my idea to get a job during vacation. When I was thirteen, I had been allowed to straighten out the storehouse of a tile manufacturer without needing any help. My mother was of the opinion that the time had come for me to face the unpleasant aspects of life. "The sooner, the better!" she said. Then I'd be armed early enough for the struggle that, at least to her mind, was life. At the age of fourteen, I stacked magazines and heat-sealed them on pallets that were delivered in vans to tobacco-and-newspaper vendors. Now, at sixteen, I helped out in the lunch-meat department of the supermarket where I had worked for six weeks last summer.

I slid out of the sickroom atmosphere of the seven-o'clock bus only to be taken into a different kind of custody. The moment I used my employees' card for the purpose of releasing the security device on the delivery entrance, I had joined in a process of breathless urgency to which everybody – department head no less than trainee – had to pay tribute: the fact that one always got there one second late. I had hardly put on my white work coat and my little paper hat with its red-and-white stripes than I heard a "why hasn't the bread been taken out of the freezer?" I had barely hurried to the freezer in order to stack the bread, which was wrapped in airtight plastic wrap and hard as a brick, in a shopping cart and pushed it toward the sales booth where I would have to arrange it on a coated baking sheet and push it into the oven, than I was slapped in the back of my neck with a "why isn't the bread in the oven yet?" I had the feeling that I needed to adjust my movements, the rhythms of my breathing and of my heartbeat to a clock that was ticking too fast. This ticking turned into a clanking as the day went on, which made me think that I had gone back to the machine at which I had been sitting a year ago with plugs in my ears, punching the manufacturer's name into little pieces of metal.

The supermarket, though frequented by hundreds of people coming and leaving every hour, was almost completely cut off from the outside world. A breath of wintry air would squeeze in through the tinted Plexiglas door that would part automatically the moment something approached it, and then would dissipate after a few seconds where the row of chained-together shopping carts was blocking its further advance. There was no window even in the room where we took our breaks or in that section of the storage facility to which the sales personnel had access. Air was blown into the store by a humming climate-control system, and a nervous kind of light was provided by neon tubes which made the place look like an operating room, seeming to put an electric charge into the chips bags, ravioli cans and jam glasses. The tension emanating from their glittering colors spread to one's own work until one had developed a nearly personal aversion to every single bit of olive in a slice of mortadella.

Herr Schwarz, the department head, was satisfied with us. Company policy which promoted the acceleration of work – more from fewer associates in less time – was written in such a way as to leave us no time in the first place to find out if there was something we could say to each other. The photocopied handouts the store manager had distributed after closing time and which demanded that during work time one should refrain from any comment that was not work-related, were basically pointless.

The customer annulled all work rules. He was king. In order to satisfy the wishes of His Majesty, one could desert any work ordered by the branch manager and if necessary – greatest taboo of all – leave the building during work hours. Even though I had been hired to compensate for the absence of colleagues who in February were taking a leave from serving the customer and hit the ski slopes, I tried to avoid this very service as much as I possibly could. Herr Schwarz had told me on the very first day that customers loved to reprimand rookies who were still slow and not quite so dexterous. Some older regular customers, for example, would only talk to Herr Schwarz while leading any other associate through the lunch–meat counter by pointing with their index fingers and nodding their heads.

Associates who had been working in this store for years had so coordinated their every movement that their gaze, faraway in any case, would completely get lost in the farther reaches of a shelf as they were moving the packages, bottles and cans whose expiration dates were approaching to the front and arranging new ones in back. For years they had stayed the same, except for an increase around their waists and a more distinct appearance of their varicose veins. As far back as the colleagues could remember, the moistened wreath of hair was all there is to their coiffure, or the "no problem" sign in their faces marked the spot where no one expected any longer to notice the emergence of a smile. They knew everything about everybody. Their robot-like way of working allowed them to devote their attention to processes other than those their hands were presently engaged in. Their ears were inexplicably attuned to picking up anything colleague X may be whispering to her colleague Y in the next aisle, even as they were being bombarded with the music of popular hits and the announcement of specials that were constantly coming over the loudspeakers.

The supermarket was a company training center. Its work force was being augmented by associates from all corners of the country who brought a surfeit of good humor with them because they considered their training period a time of paid vacation. To go out drinking with them after closing time had the inestimable advantage that one would never meet them again and that the far-fetched stories one would tell, the suggestive gestures, unbuttoned blouse and the hand inside it had no future, no consequences.

One day I found myself riding a merry-go-round at the conclusion of such an evening of hard drinking, with a heavy stone on my tongue and sitting in the fetal position on the passenger side of Christa's car – she was the assistant manager. She had hit the curb and come to a stop in the middle of the street. "Doesn't do a damn bit of good!" she said, perhaps merely referring to her son who, to quote her own words, had more fat on him than the entire selection of our meat department was able to offer, and whom she had been sending to weight-loss and special-diet clinics for years.

I came to slowly, trying to straighten myself and with that movement hitting my head against her knee. I tried to contemplate whether to kiss the inside of her upper thigh or to be careful that I didn't throw up on her. She made the decision for me by kicking my temple with her knee: "What's that? Want to spend the night?"

The night had been as casual as an insurance salesman who moves in close and opens his fake-leather briefcase unasked; but now it had become overcast. Every word that one said, every move of the hand that one performed would first of all signify that one had not jumped off this night express while there was still time. The chance that we might do it in the car was nil. For that, Christa would have to be a different person. Someone who would be glad about the unpredictable turns an event might take. Christa, however, swallowed things of this sort like pills – she didn't care for the side effects.

In a few hours she would be back behind the glass counter – her movements, her facial expressions would give no clue that she was feeling a whole night of drinking in her bones. She had appropriated the company's image of what a human body was. The best specimen was a body that was kept in motion to such an extent that the mind could not keep up with it. If there was no place where a moment of thinking might catch up with her pain, her doubt, then such an idea might never arise in the first place. At least that was what Christa tried to make herself believe when she wrapped the cheese for the second time in a fresh piece of plastic wrap or when she polished the squeaky-clean glass display case so as to banish the thought that she might need a moment of rest. If an emergency situation evolved after all, when there was nothing to do, when no customers were waiting, when all the lunch meat had been sliced in advance and the floor had been scrubbed, there was nothing left for Christa to do but play with herself, bite her fingernails, or, with her legs bopping, gnash her teeth and hurry through a daydream until an "are you working here?" would give her a start. She could almost frighten a customer with her will to be of service.

 I tried to open the car door and get out, which ended with my falling asleep again. I awakened amid a confusion of loud music, of yelling, of a half-full bottle being passed around, of being grabbed by hands that belonged to colleagues from the market who could enunciate what they were trying to say to me only with a good admixture of saliva. I wanted nothing but to keep sleeping and for this purpose to turn the radio off, until I realized that the music was in fact coming from a beer joint and I was no longer sitting in the car but was hanging in the air, horizontally, and being carried into this place.

 I slipped out of the hands of those carrying me who made no attempt, however, to stop my fall. None of them bent his knee, none his back to grab me by the arm before I hit the ground. After my head struck the sidewalk and I had straightened out again, I looked into laughing faces. Fury rose inside me but collapsed the next moment. The cold morning air that tickled the mucous membranes in my nose and the edge of my gums allowed me to perceive that all of them had to go to work while I could basically go home whenever I felt like it.

 For a moment, the world stood upside down: They, in point of fact, were down on the ground, while I had the last laugh.

Self-Circumcision

I WAS STILL WORKING on my beef casserole when my mother who had started cleaning the table planted herself next to me. "Off, or not off?" she asked. In one hand she held a thick string of her hair, in the other a pair of scissors. I shrugged my shoulders. She put both hands behind her neck and, bending her back, scooped her hair forward so that it fell down full length, almost touching the floor. In the light of the lamp over our dining table I saw to what extent age had taken up position on her head and had raised the gray flag. She was thirty-nine. For a moment I imagined her being a wax figure who had turned into a fixture in the television room of a retirement home, and who had left the world of emotions behind for good – something she claimed off and on she was looking forward to. "You need to color the roots." She went into the vestibule, came back after a while and again planted herself next to me: "Off, or not off."

A glass broke to pieces as she was doing the dishes. "Shit, damn it!" she hissed. "Damn it all!" For some time now she had been in the grip of an inexplicable anger against the accessories in the apartment. There wasn't a thing she didn't tear at and handle nervously and she got furious every time things broke when she manhandled them. In a certain way she had been disappointed about them as one would normally be only about a particular person.

She was talking over and over about how much she hated those rags, as she called her dresses, until one Friday evening she had emptied her closets and had sold their contents by Saturday noon to second-hand stores. She was beaming like some one who in one fell swoop had managed to come free of all bad habits. Early in the evening she was sitting in front of an empty champagne bottle and a full ashtray. "I have sold my memories," she said.

"Good Heavens!" I said to her one day. "You act like you're not going on forty, but on sixty." "When women turn forty, it's like when a man turns sixty," she said.

During my senior year in high school I was hardly ever home in the evening. My mother did not reprimand me for it. So long as there were no problems in school, I was allowed to come and go as I pleased. With her arms folded, she would lean against the frame of the bathroom door and watch me get ready for some party. Whatever I may be doing, shaving, fixing my hair, applying acne cream, her glances would sometimes burn holes into the part of my body I had just touched with my hand, as if a smirk was lurking around the corners of her mouth waiting for the right moment to let me know what a little boy I still was, all things considered. Another time she paid no attention to what I was doing but kept daydreaming and probably did not see me so much as herself at my age. As I came out of the bathroom, she didn't step aside to let me pass. It seemed as though she wanted me to leave my scent on her the way an animal does on a bush.

The less we saw of one another, the more she began to fabricate our history and to speak to me of the curse that was weighing upon us. "Whoever is born into a family like ours must be glad to come out alive." Referring to the fate of other inmates in that closed-off section as which her childhood would have to appear to me if I went by her stories, she tried to make me see how lucky I had been. "In my time, unwanted children were simply dropped off in front of a nunnery."

Most of the time she was asleep when I came home after midnight. The next day, as I entered the living room, it seemed as though she had left everything standing and lying around for no other reason than to allow me to read in the book of her evening. One time there was an empty whiskey glass next to a burned-down candle on the tinted glass plate of the little coffee table. On the adjacent sofa lay a folder with photocopies – patterns from an adult education course in silk painting she had paid for last semester but attended only once. Another time, two half-full champagne glasses were standing in front of a small mole hill made of white cigarette and brown cigarillo butts. Their trail of moist and dried spots led across the sofa to an opened television guide in which my mother had marked a program so firmly with a ball-point pen that the paper was torn at that place.

On the few evenings when I stayed home, everything – plates, glasses, bones, orange peels – was immediately cleared away, washed off and thrown out, the table cloth changed, even the rug under the dining table straightened. My mother didn't have to say it but the conciliatory glimmer in her eyes gave clear indication that the crepuscular misfortune lurking in a world of shady purposes to pounce on us would retreat into its cave if all around us there was nothing but glimmer and glitter.

She started to go through her collection of photos and to let me look, as if she didn't notice, at the contents of those drawers in her desk that had until now been off limits to me. I was surprised to see the many pictures from the time of her youth that showed her being happy. I discovered a photo of her in a bikini with two boys carrying her on their shoulders. Her arms were stretched out forward as if to take in a whole world – or at least a different kind of life. Another picture showed her with my grandmother, the two of them close to falling down with laughter in the middle of the street. "That was when I put so much make-up on her and fixed her hair so that nobody recognized her as we were walking through the village. I told everybody she was a cousin from Klagenfurt. We did have good times, in those days." There were pictures of me standing in my walker under the chestnut tree or sitting on a blanket in the orchard, growing like a pear in the sun. In some of these pictures there were men standing next to me or my grandmother who didn't quite know why they needed to be in the picture that was being taken. Their faces would change over the years as frequently as the size of my mother's sun glasses and handbags.

From a certain time on, the photos looked more and more like pictures taken for an art-deco magazine in which she – wearing nothing but a silver fox draped around her body – along with all the other precious objects underlined the exquisite taste of the apartment's proprietor. Finally, photos displaying her on her canopied bed in unmistakable poses. "I am sure you can take it," she said, winking at me. She was naked, with her eyes shut and her tongue licking her lips. She had spread her legs and was closing her hands around her knees. Her tense belly looked like a sandstone-colored surface into which red lines had been carved. The part of the picture that would have shown her vagina had fallen victim to an act of censorship that was enforced ten years after the photo had been taken. She had used scissors and cut off a small, intimate part of herself. There had come a time, she said, when she could not look at herself like that any longer.

She was sitting next to me on the sofa. The way she

had crossed her legs and rested one arm on the back of the sofa let me know how much she was intent on letting me feel that it was perfectly natural for us to be looking at photos like these together. It hadn't been her purpose to surprise, much less to shock me. Rather, she wanted to make me curious again about herself. Consequently, when I picked up a little sliver from a photo that was about the size of a small postage stamp, I felt a jolt go through her body. The cloth of her dress didn't tighten, she neither held her breath nor looked at me with her eyes wide open. But there was something of the tension created by a detective story in the air. Was it not too late to catch me? Did I make the same mistakes twice? Did I return to the scene of the crime again?

I stared at the sliver I held between the thumb and index finger of my right hand. My mother was nothing but a pulsating sensorium of nerves, pores and little hairs that were exploring my body and the space surrounding it for the purpose of finding out which emotions her uncovered labia in my hand were evoking in me, which emotions she herself was still able to evoke in me. It was one of her last attempts to get me to drop, as she called it, "the mask of pubescent indifference" and admit to myself and to her that everything in my life was in fact still revolving around her.

I would by now let things of this sort pass without getting all upset about them. I stood up and tossed the paper vagina among the other photos, seeing to it that I did not inadvertently make a move she had recently called the only type of emotion I was willing to permit myself in her presence – a gesture of fending off. Not even that much did I want to grant her. I said that I was going to meet somebody. Before leaving the apartment, I cast a final brief glance at her through the narrow slit left open by the living-room door. She was still sitting on the sofa, staring into a void. She felt my presence instantaneously. "When will you be back?" she asked. At such moments the wheel of time was turning back by years and I saw not my mother but myself lying on the couch in my pajamas and watching her blow me a kiss as she was leaving. Our roles had been reversed. It came as a surprise to me that I felt compassion for her – perhaps because I knew so well the fate she appeared to see coming her way from now on.

She did not cut off her hair. Instead, she shut down a different source of her erotic appeal; she kept her mouth closed. The mouth, she had explained to me at one time, must never be opened too far, or else one would be in danger of looking cheap. It was to be not more than ajar so as merely to suggest what one had to offer, rather than announce it with a fishwife's loudness. She was convinced that woman must always remain an enigma to man. Men were like children and would soon be bored with their toy.

This slit between her lips which had helped, or so she believed, to make clients who charged into the office in a fit of anger come to their senses; to mollify the principal who confronted her with repeated complaints about my behavior in class; to have the super do repairs he was under no obligation to do and do them free of charge – this slit had disappeared now, and her mouth had turned into a lipstick-red minus sign in her face.

Which does not mean that she kept completely silent. She did go on trying to find out more from me and telling about herself than I found tolerable. But her words were colored by the crape of a voice that let you hear how much she had become resigned to my not listening to her most of the time, much less giving her a satisfactory answer.

It seemed as though she had accepted the way things were going. I was convinced, however, that she would much rather have fought against it, had she known how. She did not have a really good girlfriend whose advice in such things she might have asked. She only had colleagues with whom she would sometimes go out for a glass of wine after work or do group exercises. Women avoided her. "I could throw up when I hear the word bosom buddy," she would say defiantly. Her dry analysis of the problem postulated that women who lived in steady relationships did not want to lead their partners into unnecessary temptations, whereas women who were aching for a steady relationship or had considered merely a one-night-stand, could not, in their search for an adequate partner, find a more disadvantageous companion than my mother.

One day she came home with a bouquet of bluebells. "Where did you find these?" Hesitating, almost bashful, she answered: "In the woods. I went for a walk. By myself." And, after a while: "It was just beautiful." It was only at this moment that I noticed something I should have been able to see all along if I had not been ever so busy ignoring my mother's presence: the colors of the woods had been admitted into her wardrobe. Up to the age of thirty she covered herself with the neon colors of a disco, thereafter in the dark satin and the golden trim of an opera box. Now she was wearing a dark-green lederhose and a brown jacket – old moss and autumnal foliage. Colors she had until then strictly refused to wear – not the least because they were the colors associated with the traditional costumes of the region from which we came, and therefore also the colors of the time when my grandfather would at all hours of the morning harness the horses to his wagon and go wood hauling.

The bluebells she was holding against her belly did

not as yet ring in a second springtime for her but perhaps the beginning of a phase in which her feared loss of present time would be balanced by a gain in time past – of a past that would no longer have to be adjusted to the needs of this present.

She took a single bluebell from her bouquet and held it out to me. "For you. Anyway." When I reached for the flower, our fingertips touched.

Tita

I WOKE with a stabbing pain in my bladder. My tongue was a dried-out cocoon. I was desperate to take a leak and get a drink. The others were still asleep. They were spread across the room like pieces of clothing that were left lying around wherever somebody just happened to drop them. Some of the kids were crouched into narrow armchairs, the others had shagged out on the floor. Their heads rested on the bolsters of their bent arms, among crumbs of chips, empty bottles and crushed cigarette packs. Herwig lay in the door to the bathroom. I tried to take a big step across him but came down on his fingers. He didn't move. As I was peeing into the toilet bowl beside him, the dark-yellow color of the urine brought back to my memory the half bottle of tequila in my blood so that I lost my balance and left a semicircle of urine drops on Herwig's jacket. I fought against having the residual alcohol wash my pupils out and push me again into seeing things through *its* eyes. The air tasted like plastic wrap. I tried to see clearly and moved my hand back and forth in front of my face like a windshield wiper. I recognized the outlines of an unmistakable smile: Tita. "I got to go too," she said. I was sober in no time. Herwig's body was like a wet cotton sweater. I couldn't manage to drag him away from the door. So I just posted myself in front of the toilet and watched that nobody could bother Tita and take a peek at her thighs while she whizzed.

I heard the toilet paper scrape against the aluminum lid as it was being torn off and crumpled up. I yawned loudly and made a noise to suggest how drunk I still was so that I wouldn't have to overhear her wiping her pussy. When she was anywhere near me, I was nothing but a little plot of meadow anyway on which her words and gestures bloomed like flowers – only that they had been changed inside me and were no longer referring to something at school or about her parents but to us. Her glances were butterflies, the sway of her hips was like an overarching electric guitar solo, the mere fact of her existence was a contradiction to everything my mother kept denigrating as life. I was in love for the first time.

And for all that, I barely knew her. She attended a private boarding school for girls but thank God did not live in the dormitory. I had met her one morning when I woke up next to her in a bed. We had apparently taken the wrong way out of a party, had passed out and slept without waking through the third period at school. Instead of being alarmed about his, we laughed until we, separately, discovered that we were naked under the bed cover. We couldn't remember anything and had to laugh again as we watched one another checking ourselves under the blanket to make sure that nothing had happened. Any little sign of embarrassment or shame that would tend to arise whenever a boy and a girl met during daytime and with nobody else around, had been nipped in the bud.

When she was ready to get up, she tried to pull her underwear close to the bed with her toe. Perhaps I thought that I could impress her: I got up, walked around the bed and picked her slip up. When she took it from my hand and our fingers touched on top of her panties, my penis twitched so that I – probably blushing – retreated at once. I went back to lie down and didn't turn around to look at her as she was getting up. It was quite unlike anything that usually happens at a party when one would make a move on a drunk girl and, without wasting any time over it, feel her up and down thinking: "Let's just hope this doesn't make her fall in love with me." The girls in our school, most of whom came from good families, and even more so the other girls from the private school made you feel they were wrapped in tissue paper like a present. So ready for use, so absolutely left in the dark. Since they never really knew how far they ought to go, life for many of them was full of frightful seconds, full of sudden stops.

Nothing had apparently changed for Tita. She got dressed, waved at me and left. When I was back home and looked in the mirror, I knew that this would henceforth be merely an unsatisfying substitute for her eyes. My mother was putting rollers in her hair. I knew that I must not tell her about Tita. "Sex is cheap," was her latest assertion. As a child, she said, she had watched farm hands slab pig's lard into a knothole, and do it with cows. "That's all it ever amounts to. This cheap in-out." I could almost feel her straining her ears and waiting for me to contradict her and reveal something about myself. The very next day I got Tita's phone number and used an excuse to give her a call. When she picked up the receiver, my voice deserted me.

I hoped Tita would understand it was no coincidence that again the two of us had woken up at the same time before anyone else had. If we ought to go buy rolls, she asked. "No." My refusal did not seem to surprise her. "What then?"

Herwig's parents' house was near an avenue of chestnut trees, the morning's frost still stored in their branches. This gave us goose pimples and we took off before long. But not until Tita had spent some time playing with a dog who was jumping up at her tirelessly and was hanging on to her waistband with his teeth, which didn't appear to bother her in the least. She paid as little attention to the loud shouting of the dog's owner as the animal did. When I saw its muzzle and stretched-out paws shoot up toward her face that hovered above it smiling, I thought I was little more than the tree shadow surrounding her – more clearly than ever before did I feel the existence of large white areas on the map of my emotional world and for a second could have used my hands to squash the beast that made me realize this.

An hour later I kissed her in a café in front of the other customers. I was surprised by the intensity with which she pressed my head against hers and returned my kiss. While it had been my original intention to sweep her off her feet, it was now I who was perplexed and who let everybody see his unexpected, perhaps even his undeserved happiness. She had to be home for lunch. Why didn't I come along? We crossed a bridge, its four lanes barely able to accommodate the flow of traffic. But the Yes! and No! of the engines, the clutch and release of brakes and the squawking jostle of honking horns didn't bother me. Her head was leaning against my shoulder. From the beginning I was tormented by the thought that from one day to the next she might revoke my right to caress her and hold her in my arms. Since my grandmother's death, Tita was the first person I wanted to touch this way.

Tita's mother welcomed me as though I had been coming and going in their house for quite some time. She extended her lower arm toward me, little lumps of soil sprouting from her hands like fish scales. She spent most of her time in the garden. From Tita's window one could watch her sowing, watering, pulling weeds, trimming and fertilizing. She was from the country, the same as I. Work was an inner need for her. It did not age her but kept her young even though her hair had turned gray and she never used fingernail polish and lipstick to underline the impression of youthfulness. Tita's father worked for an architectural firm. Sometimes he would show up for lunch and with quick lunch-break gestures subdivide the table into grid squares. He made it a habit to interrupt his wife in mid-sentence. The kiss he planted on her cheek as he returned to work anticipated the noise of the door he slammed on his way out the next moment.

    I was disappointed not to find a new home in Tita's room, one to which I might be able to go after school, or in which I could have spent every night. The things in her room were laced together by invisible threads and formed a miniature world from which I was excluded. When her parents had an argument, or she had a problem at school, or her body changed in a way that confused her, she sought refuge in her room. As with television where lunacy and senselessness could presumably be terminated with a click of the button, a feeling of security and confidence returned to her as soon as she was surrounded by her plush giraffes, scented candles, little bouquets of dried roses and enamel jewelry boxes. They were freighted with remembrances I had no way of bypassing. I didn't want Tita to tell me what she had found where and been given by whom. She herself was able to transform herself into one of these things, which would make her appear as though she were shrouded in waxen foil. She would be impervious to any kind of touch – which revealed the extent of absence her body was able to communicate. For a long time I was not able to sleep with her in her room. Until recently I had no choice but to do the unthinkable: I had to take her home with me.

    When we were lying in my bed naked, I had the feeling that a promise given a long time ago had been honored. Her dark hair, lashes and eyebrows were pieces of attire as light as insects and fitting me perfectly. My hands made a survey of the square centimeters of her body that were hidden between folds of skin. I dived head first beneath the bed cover. A sultry breeze let my nerve ends, pores and particles feel a foretaste of what to expect. Even before my eyes did, my tongue and my lips gained a comprehensive impression of those heights and depths I hoped would become my new home. I was careful not to speak to Tita in these terms for fear that the undeniable measure of desperation reverberating in such words might frighten her off.

    I hoped that sex would contribute to making her feel for me what I felt for her. Tita had started moving my foreskin back and forth, which I found repulsive because it made me think of masturbation – a situation in which I found myself on the one side of a high wall and the rest of humanity on the other. Tita sensed this immediately and stopped. It was also she who pulled the cover off of us. My dull thoughts glimmered on her body. Then she lay on her back: "Come."

    When I penetrated her and moved inside her, I had no idea how hard I should thrust. I thought of her room and that it would be best not to leave any part of the wall standing. That's exactly how I proceeded inside her vagina – as if the force of my thrusts could extinguish everything that had been before. With the hectic speed of a billiard player who is shooting to beat the clock, I thrust my penis into her hole again and again. "Not so rough," she said at last. From then on it was she who set the tempo – either by screaming it out as if in a market hall, or by whispering it in my ear, or by gently leaning on her elbows and by moving her groin in sync with mine. I fucked her and, as it were, hovered above her, in a rare balance of doing and observing – until I filtered from her groans the sound of a key turning in the lock of the apartment door. At that very same moment I knew that it had been a mistake to ask my mother if she was in fact going to the art-show opening after work. She had no doubt become suspicious right away. For too long I had shown no interest in how she spent her evenings. And even though she had said that she was going to, I am sure she had decided that very moment to come home and check what was taking place there.

I tried to pull out of Tita and pick the cover up off the floor. She had closed her eyes and was oblivious to all of this. I was close to interrupting it in mid-course – and yet went on. I didn't care if my mother was watching us.

As my semen was spreading through Tita like foaming light, I thought I could feel my mother's dark gaze following it on its way – a gaze that was fierce enough to drill through human flesh the way a toothpick goes through a slice of cheese or an olive, and which this time had no other choice but to retreat so that I would not have to turn around and untangle myself from Tita's kiss. I felt like a newborn, red in the face and gasping for life. Along with my sweat also my mother's existential struggle had dripped off of me, that infertile sac which had apparently been overlooked at my birth and had not been removed.

Afterword

by Michael Winkler

Now that the account of his early years has come to an end we may have been swayed to sympathize, if not to identify with its scuffling and tousled young hero who has at last broken free and asserted his independence. The reason for our shifting though increasingly empathetic involvement with his story may be the impression that it has been told with passionate intensity and therefore with personal truthfulness. Even scenes that appear distorted by a perfervid imagination exude the assurance of authenticity, of an essential objectivity whose harsh details are somewhat softened by a poetic sheen. Nonetheless, they also must represent, we feel, real-life experiences and spontaneous perceptions that have retained, even a good many years later, their original status as facts and firsthand knowledge. It seems that the author has used a nameless "I" to describe the circumstances of his own life accurately and through precisely evoked details. Peter Truschner, in other words, has written the autobiography of his infancy with his grandparents in a Carinthian farming village and of his turbulent teenage years with his mother in Salzburg.

Schlangenkind is a novel, of course, a self-conscious construct of life's elements. As such it is a product of the aesthetic imagination. Whatever hard core of facts, centered in personal experience or identifiable as the irreducible givens of the social sphere, may have crossed over into its domain, can no longer be verified, if that means: checked and proved to be accurate or fabricated.

Measured by such expectations, very little of what makes up this book may be true, or, to put it differently, the truth of artistic fiction is always stranger than the facts of life because creative writers reject the injunction to "write about what they know" and instead follow their imagination. In remarks included in a review of his book by Joachim Scholl and broadcast on the program "Büchermarkt" of the radio network Deutschlandfunk (January 25, 2001), Truschner said that his original plan had been to write merely an autobiographical novella about his grandparents. "But all of a sudden I found myself looking into a hole because the story balked at the way I had tried to write it alongside my own biography. Its characters started to develop a life of their own, a biography inside the as yet unwritten novel, and that's what I had to do for them from that moment on. What followed is all pure invention." One purpose of this emancipation from the demands exerted by factual reality is the desire to stimulate curiosity and to *provoke* experiences, not to replicate them.

As a novelist, Truschner can dispense with the customary disclaimer that "the names, places, characters, and incidents" depicted in this work "are the products of the author's imagination or are used fictitiously." They do not, by their very nature as fiction, purport to portray a particular small segment of Austrian society roughly a generation ago – there are hints at an internal time frame but only a handful of historical dates – and of a specific individual's precarious place in it. The author's intent is not social criticism by way of exposing what Flaubert in the title of *Madame Bovary* (1857) had called "Moeurs de Province." Otherwise, his readers would be justified in asking for a little more documentary proof. He also is not interested in psychological analysis, especially not of the kind that focuses on "the lack of a nurturing environment" or on "the lurid fascination with sexual perversities" or on "juvenile narcissism and revenge fantasies," etc. Material for such clinical investigations can no doubt be found in every chapter but whoever has found it was looking in the wrong place.

It would not only be condescending but a fundamental misreading of genuine literature to credit the author with a highly subjective believability and then to attribute the "flamboyant pyrotechnics" of his metaphorical language to an easily excitable self-indulgence in raw emotions, American style. Their "theatricality" would, consequently, have to be excused as being integral to the conventions that constitute the "nonconformity" of (currently fashion-able) confessional literature; its eccentricities, whether hilarious or annoying, may then have to be tolerated as the violent eruptions of a traumatized identity in need of some sort of talk-and-scream therapy. And so now we analyze the author through his fictional inventions, oblivious to the fact, for example, that *his* facility with words contradicts *their* reticence and distrust of them, both spoken and written, quite in contrast to their reliance on expressive body language that signals rapport as often as it gets out of hand, as it were, to the point where physical confrontation strangles dialogue.

Perhaps paradoxically it is the narrator's retrospective detachment from his characters, it is his cerebral distance – one might call it a reptilian coldbloodedness – that heightens the emotional impact of his story. Truschner himself, in the interview mentioned above, put it this way: " . . . the child, of course, wants to be a part of what's going on, above all of sensual, of direct and 'hands-on' physical processes. But at the same time he withdraws, steps back; and that was my challenge: can it be done successfully, in aesthetic terms, to keep these two aspects side by side and the one a part of the other, to sustain them in one metaphor, in one sentence, in one chapter: sensual spontaneity and, simultaneously, distance and mental awareness of this immediacy." The issue, in other words, is how to establish appropriate perspectives. And that is an aesthetic difficulty, which shows intelligent literature to evolve from an *imaginative process of thinking*. Such a premise may redirect our customary preoccupation with ideas and themes toward the way human relationships, and not only those involving power and abusive behavior, are structured. That means, how points of view as positions from which to see things and people, directly and close-up or obliquely and at second hand, are set up and rearranged to signify differences of nearness and remove and to suggest (rather than spell out) the pain in attempts to overcome them.

Close attention to the artistic strategies that seek to guide the reader's perception is especially pertinent to how we respond to the scenes involving sexual acts. Some of these may strike us at first sight as examples of vulgar sensationalism, and, for example in the penultimate chapter "Self-Circumcision," as a pornographic combina-tion of pathetic exhibitionism and voyeuristic cool. But we should look beyond that crude surface reality, recognizing the ambivalent implications of this "self-mutilation" as another metaphoric act and noticing its suggestive use of (what linguists call) the sememe "lips": In a last and desperate attempt to hold on to her son the aging mother once more shows herself naked and at the same time excises the old focus of her pictures, which are the outward evidence of her life retained as memory, so that she can live now with a different image of herself – a transformation no less liberating than her son's final shedding of his old skin. Her

"Selbstbeschneidung" then implies, after a lifetime of disappointed expectations and of abuse at the hands of others, a turn toward "Selbst-bescheidung," as to a modesty chosen, albeit resignedly, by herself. Fictional characters, unless they themselves "read" their lives and the world surrounding them as "texts," realize only at moments of epiphany what the reader should constantly keep in mind: that they are performing metaphorical acts whose distinctive linkage into a network of meaningful signs and signals establishes the aesthetic validity of the work of art. In that case Truschner's novel is a novel *sui generis*, one that self-consciously defies being absorbed into a general category. It specifically contravenes that tradition which has been called the "Hohe Tauern" of postwar Austrian literature, i. e., that long and diverse list of books that seek to come to terms with the various "brutalities" and the deprivations that life in the country can inflict on a sensitive person.

Peter Truschner was born in Klagenfurt in 1967 and grew up in nearby Maria Saal, a historical little town in an attractive countryside. Tourists will likely experience it both as picturesque and hospitable, local youngsters without private transportation may easily find it depressing. Thomas Bernhard had lived there for a while by choice, the dramatist Peter Turrini, a native son, couldn't get out fast enough. Truschner, though referring more to a mood in his book than to a specific locality, felt in rural disorder a "wonderful, mysterious vagueness that works against chaos whereas in the city there exists a very efficiently ordered categorization of everything that works according to firm rules" – even in Austria. As a university student in Salzburg he took courses in philosophy, political science, and media studies but apparently not in literary criticism and without finishing a degree. He mentions Robert Musil's shorter fiction and Harold Brodkey, Sylvia Plath, and Vladimir Nabokov as exemplary for his education in the art and craft of fiction writing. In 1990 he started publishing reviews, essays, and stories in various journals. His play *Plexiglaswelten* (Plexiglass worlds) was performed at the Toihaus-Theater in Salzburg in 1997 (published 1998), a "Dramolett" titled *Fasching* (Mardi gras) written for its "Kinder- und Jugendtheaterfestival Teatro," followed in 2000, and a new play *Man kann, also muß man* (One can, and so one must) was finished in 2003. In 1999 Truschner moved to Berlin.

His talent was recognized early and rewarded with prestigious prizes: Austria's State Stipend for Literature in 1999; the Prize of the Federal Chancellor's Office for a first work in literature, and a stipend to live at "Künstlerdorf" [artists village] Schöppingen, a German foundation, in 2001; the Grant-in-Aid [Förderpreis] of the Province of Carinthia, and the "Jahresstipendium" of the Austrian "Literatur-Mechana" in 2002; and a year's residence at the International Artists House "Villa Concordia" in Bamberg in 2004/2005.

I am grateful to Drs. Christa Gaug and Maria-Regina Kecht, both of Rice University, for help with some Austrian locutions I could not find in any dictionary.

SERPENT'S CHILD is a coming-of-age novel that is set in a farming village near Klagenfurt and in Salzburg during the later 1970s. Its sure sense of place and time and its psychological acuity suggest the intimacy of autobiographical experience that knows how traditions of patriarchal abuse and the dictates of conformity disfigure a seemingly idyllic milieu. A person of inquisitive intelligence, Truschner's protagonist observes the dynamics of dysfunctional relationships with, by turns, the dispassionate objectivity of an outsider and the tenderness of a wounded, disoriented sensitivity in search of human closeness. His story is told as a fast-paced sequence of interconnected episodes, some brief and self-contained, others recaptured at later moments and expanded in new directions as perspectives shift and attitudes and insights change. It is a vivid account, forceful in its evocation of the domestic and other social details that make every one of the outrageous and endearing characters and the drama of their psychological conflicts persuasive, and at the same time restrained by a subtle sense of self-irony and compassion. Most remarkable, however, is the narrator's invention of images. His fondness for extended metaphors and analogous similes charges his language with an explosive and at times extravagant energy and thus speaks for the continued artistic vigor of a fictional genre that has been an Austrian obsession for decades.

PETER TRUSCHNER, born in Klagenfurt in 1967, grew up in Maria Saal (Carinthia) and enrolled in philosophy, political science and media studies at Salzburg University. He started publishing in various cultural and literary journals in 1990, and has also written a number of short plays. In 1999 he moved to Berlin, and during 2004/2005 was a guest at the international artists' house Villa Concordia in Bamberg (Germany). Truschner is the recipient of several other awards, among them the Austrian *Staatsstipendium* for Literature (1999). *Schlangenkind* is his first novel.

MICHAEL WINKLER has taught European literature and culture at Rice University in Houston, TX until his retirement in 2000. He has translated Gerhard Roth's novel *Der See* (1995) for Ariadne Press and (in collaboration with Edward Snow) Rainer Maria Rilke's *Diaries*. Their annotated translation of the poet's correspondence with Lou Andreas-Salomé will be published by W. W. Norton in 2005.